A YARD OF SUN

A Summer Comedy

CHRISTOPHER FRY

A YARD OF SUN

A Summer Comedy

NEW YORK

OXFORD UNIVERSITY PRESS

1970

TO
TAM AND VRELI
WITH LOVE

NOTES

page 1 'TRAGUARDO': goal.

page 74 PROVENZAN SALVANI, a Ghibelline, was chief in authority among the Sienese at the time of the battle of Montaperti (1260); and after the defeat of the Florentines he was the strongest advocate of the destruction of their city. He once humbled himself by affecting the garb and manner of a beggar in the market-place of Siena, to procure the money to ransom a friend, who was the prisoner of Charles of Anjou.

'All Tuscany rang with the sound of him . . . and now hardly is a whisper of him in Siena, whereof he was lord.' *Purgatorio*, canto xi, line 121.

page 74 LUIGI FIORENTINO, Sienese poet, b. 1913.

page 111 A NOTE ON THE PALIO. I am grateful to Mr. Stewart Perowne, and *The Times* newspaper, for permission to use this wonderfully evocative description of the event which is the background to the play.

CHARACTERS

ANGELINO BRUNO
ROBERTO
LUIGI } *his sons*
EDMONDO
GIOSETTA SCAPARE
GRAZIA, *her daughter*
ALFIO, *a jockey*
ANA-CLARA, *from Portugal*
CESARE SCAPARE

Two delivery-men, two menservants,
a chauffeur (ETTORE),
a secretary, a lady's-maid,
a photographer (PIERO MARTINI)

SCENE
The courtyard of the Palazzo del Traguardo, Siena

TIME
July 1946

ACT ONE

July 1946. The courtyard of the Palazzo del Traguardo. A gateway to the street. A handsome doorway to the grand apartment. A smaller door to an apartment partly used as an Osteria; and, across the yard, the door to a third apartment.

ANGELINO BRUNO, *a stocky, bushy-browed man of middle-age, is sweeping from the porter's room to the street outside.*

ROBERTO BRUNO, *his son, wearing an old outgrown dressing-gown, enters from the Osteria.*

ROBERTO. Don't you know it's a dirty world, father?
And every day is as dirty as another.
That's why we have to wash.

ANGELINO.   It's only nine.
I thought you'd lie with the day a bit.
What sinful hour was it when you got to bed?

ROBERTO. Five o'clock. And then it was too hot to sleep.
I need a bath. There's no water in the taps.

ANGELINO. It's been turned off at the mains.

ROBERTO.   Damn.

ANGELINO. There was a storm last night. But there you are,
What's a collision in the atmosphere to you
Once you all start singing at one of your reunions?
You think you're the thunder and the lot. At half-past eleven
The heavens emptied their pots, I can tell you.

ROBERTO. Yes, I know. Rosa Levanti came
And fetched me to her father about midnight.
The old man didn't want to die till the weather improved.

[1]

ANGELINO. Did you keep him alive?

ROBERTO.   Yes, while the storm lasted.
  Then he seemed to notice the silence: put out his hand
  As though he'd been sheltering in a doorway,
  Looked up, and made off. Just before daylight.

ANGELINO.   Still,
  You did your best, poor old Giovanni. So you knew
  The streets were flooded. It overflowed the sewers.

ROBERTO. We have no water when there's a drought, and then
  We have no water when there's a flood. You see
  The hopeless way this town is organized!

ANGELINO. What do you want?
  Everyone with snow white necks and typhoid?

ROBERTO. I want an efficient water-supply, and not
  A hackneyed parable of modern life.
  I want a shave, and a coffee, and a blessed bath.
  I don't expect to have to start the day
  On a bottle of beer.
                    [*He goes into the Osteria.* ANGELINO *raises his voice.*

ANGELINO.   It isn't believable!
  You call yourself a doctor? What a fantasy!
  I've said the flood-water floated the sewers!
  Why don't you listen? That's an Act of God
  Not a political manifesto. A doctor!
  You ought to be saying seven Hail Marys
  For not having to wade up to your gorge
  Through an epidemic. Always the same thing:
  You have a Reunion, and that's perfectly right,
  You are all fine fellows, I say it to God,
  The Partisans were all fine courageous fellows.
  You deserve to shout the night down, once a month.

[2]

But next morning you have to come back to earth
And, each time you do, the earth isn't good enough for you.
       [ROBERTO *emerges, grinning, with a glass and bottle.*

ROBERTO Is it good enough for you?

ANGELINO [*with a shrug*].   What is good enough?
You are not good enough for me, your brother
Luigi isn't good enough for me, I
Am not good enough for me. But I don't blame that
On the city fathers.

ROBERTO.   Why not? They made our environment.
They're the ones who made us in the gutter's image.

ANGELINO. And a fine assorted lot we've turned out to be.
I couldn't love us more dearly
If we were twenty-four carat. As for environment,
The environment is in for a transformation.
I'm opening up the Palazzo again. What
A delight! I can't help patting myself on the back—
Like you when the stamina of one of your patients
Pulls him through a crisis.
I've been told to expect the new owners today.

ROBERTO. Have you? Who are they?

ANGELINO.   I don't know. They must be
High quality of some kind or other.
Like God, they only reveal themselves through an agent.

ROBERTO. So we're enemy-occupied territory again;
That's a cheerful prospect.

ANGELINO.   You behave yourself!
Roberto, give me your word you'll behave decently!
If you try and start a class-vendetta
Just where I'm paid to keep the floor clear of bodies

[3]

You can move into lodgings. I'm not having it!
Fidget with your Luger in another district.

ROBERTO. Look, I was only—

ANGELINO.   Haven't I been a good father?

ROBERTO. Yes, you have been a very—

ANGELINO.   Don't perjure yourself.
I don't know what I've been. You're always saying
I've got no rules of conduct. Maybe that is
What I haven't got. I'm bound to admit
I like things to have a shine to them—
And I know the sun can lure larks with bits of tin
And pheasants with a mirror, and all that macaroni.
I won't say you're not right. But anyway
I spent all I'd got on you and Luigi
To get you where you are, and that's no further
Than a two-year-old could push you with its left hand.
Look at you, working for nothing because you refuse
To attend anybody who can afford to pay you.
I don't call that the top of the ladder. And now
You haven't enough money to treat them properly.
I suppose you think that makes you a philanthropist.
I invested my money in you because I thought
You had brains, and would make my future, you and Luigi.
But I'm farther off from a future than I ever was.
So don't make trouble when things take a lucky turn.
What do we get out of the Osteria
Except good friends drinking at our expense?
And being caretaker of this Palazzo
Doesn't take care of anything. But now
We have rich cows coming to be milked,
And they'll introduce us to other rewarding udders,
And, before you know, we have the most profitable

[4]

Restaurant in Siena. But none of this
Will happen if I've got you sniping at their haunches
From behind every shutter in the building.
Do I make you understand?

ROBERTO.   We'll have to see
How they behave.

ANGELINO.   You make me so anxious.

ROBERTO.   Why?
Don't cross your bridge till you see it collapsing.
We don't know yet that I'm going to have to shoot them.
            [*A man's voice is heard singing down the street.*
That voice could only be my brother Luigi's.

ANGELINO. Yes, I can feel it in my neck muscles.
Some people have time on their hands, but I haven't this morning.
            [*He goes in through the great doorway. The singing ends as*
            LUIGI *turns into the courtyard from the street.*

LUIGI. Good morning, Bobo!

ROBERTO.   Why do you have to exercise
That mongrel tenor in a public thoroughfare?

LUIGI. It's my part in the song of praise. If we're not equipped
To give thanks, we shouldn't give up trying. What's
The matter with you? You look like one of your patients.
A pity on the first day of a better world.

ROBERTO. A what?

LUIGI.   I remembered it as soon as it was light.
I swallowed the last black morsel of what I was dreaming
And said Here it is, we're all new men
In a new world. I stood at the window, like Adam
Looking out on the first garden.

[5]

ROBERTO.   I remember the view:
    Over the knacker's back yard.

LUIGI.   Bobo, the trouble with you is
    You only see life through a rifle-sight
    And only hear it through a stethoscope.
    You're always either killing or curing. You won't
    Allow that life ever knows her own business.
    But nevertheless there are times when she manages
    To fight her way out of our raping clutches
    And today is one of them. Not quite a virgin,
    We all know that, but at least confessed and absolved.
    I'm overjoyed to take her back.

ROBERTO.   Lucky
    Life. What do you find so parthenogenetic
    About this morning?

LUIGI.   Where's your vision of life?
    You know it's the first practice-run for the Palio—
    And you know this parish has got the best horse
    It has ever had, and the best jockey too.
    Doesn't it lift your heart to think we're behaving
    Like old times? The Palio! The first
    Since we cleared the war off our premises!

ROBERTO. So it's 'we' who did it? That's the new story?
    Have you forgotten already which side you were on?

LUIGI. No, not yet. But we were a help. We had
    The sense to lose. That deserves some credit.

ROBERTO. Does it?

LUIGI.   Yes, I think so.

ROBERTO.   You won't get it from me, then.
    I still suffer from girds of nausea

[6]

Whenever I think of the way you used to strut
In your black shirt.

LUIGI.   Well, I strut in any shirt;
I know I strut. When I was small—perhaps
You've forgotten—the teacher always used to think
I'd fouled my breeches.

ROBERTO.   When I let myself think
Of the money father wasted, entertaining
Those arm-shooting gangsters and assassins
Because you fancied yourself as a politician—
Careful money he'd taken all his life to earn—
Until he had to sell up the business,
I've so much useless anger, I could crack apart.

LUIGI. Or smash me against the wall. I wish you would.
I'm sick of watching you master the temptation.
Then we might forget it. I've admitted,
Until I'm hoarse, it was a false start.
But I was the one set back by it.

ROBERTO.   Just you?
I set out to be a healer not a killer.
It was what you tried to stand for made me lethal.

LUIGI. Yes, well; we're out of it now. No good pining.
Where's daddo? Eh? Where is he?

ROBERTO.   Opening up
The Palazzo.

LUIGI.   Has somebody taken it?
Yes? There, you see, what did I tell you?
It's the day of bright beginnings. Just as I said.
            [ANGELINO *throws open an upper window.* LUIGI *shouts
            up to him.*

[7]

That's right, daddo! Open the doors and windows!
Let the sun decontaminate the place,
Let the air get rid of that fug of requisitioning.
Who are they, these people?

ROBERTO.   He doesn't know.
The children of Mammon come back for their broken toys,
The first of the swarm. That's what it sounds like.

LUIGI. They're going to think they're in the black-bear country
If they see much of you.

ROBERTO.   Somebody's got to protect him.
The more he's exploited, the more he glows with pride.
You made the most of that. And if you thought
There was anything left you'd be fastening on him again
To launch you on your Christian Democrat cruise.
That mine's worked out.

LUIGI.   You are an unforgiving
Unfair bastard! Why am I supposed
To be the particularly guilty one?
Because eight years ago I put on a dirty shirt?
He spent no more on me than he spent on you.
And if our brother Edmondo hadn't imagined
He could take on the world alone with his bare wits
He would have had *his* share as well.

ANGELINO [*entering*].   Enough,
That's enough, Luigi! I won't have his name mentioned,
You know that.

LUIGI.   Yes, I know, but I was only
Standing up for myself against slander and calumny.
I was saying that if Edmondo had wanted—

ANGELINO.   Luigi!
Will you keep quiet when I tell you that's enough?

[8]

There's no such name in our family. I don't remember him.
Where is Grazia this morning?

ROBERTO.   That's the way!
Don't let memory interfere with your pleasures,
Either of you. Ignore the uncomfortable.

ANGELINO. Luigi, why did you have to pick this morning
To argue with him? He's had no bath or coffee.
And last night was a Partisan Reunion.
Even the sunlight scratches him.

LUIGI.   Argue? Me?
I came here dispensing drops of light
Like a wet retriever. If it's water he wants
They're coming along the road with it now. I saw them
Dumping it off in churns.

> [ANGELINO *shouts up to an opposite window.*

ANGELINO.   Grazia Scapare!
Grazia!—I wish someone would teach her that time
Promises far more than it lives up to.
She thinks eternal life is one of the basic
Human rights, a kind of public swimming bath.
But I wouldn't lose her an hour of those few years
When we seem to be living for ever.

LUIGI [*to* ROBERTO].   You've made me thirsty,
You tup, sweating to defend myself.

> [*He goes into the Osteria as* GIOSETTA, GRAZIA's *mother,
> comes out of her apartment and hangs rugs on a line.*

GIOSETTA. Good-morning. What's all the shouting for?

ANGELINO.   Your daughter,
Where's your daughter?

[9]

GIOSETTA.   I sent her to buy some bread,
  But that was an hour ago at least. I'm sure
  I can't tell you what she has done with herself.

ANGELINO. She was going to help me get the Palazzo ready.

ROBERTO. Don't you know, Giosetta?—we're supposed to have
  Our tongues at the ready to lick the boots of the great ones.

GIOSETTA. The shame of it.

ROBERTO [*shrugging*].   We're all well used to blushing.
                    [LUIGI *returns, opening a bottle of beer.*

LUIGI. Though not all of us blush so red. Here's Grazia.
        [GRAZIA *has appeared in the street outside, with* ALFIO,
        *a young man pushing a Vespa. He props it against a wall
        within the archway.*

GIOSETTA. Here she is.

ANGELINO.   Ah, here she is!

GRAZIA.   Good-morning.
  Why are you all saying I am here? Has something
  Happened?

ANGELINO.   Who said she was going to come over early
  And make the place glisten?

GRAZIA [*making for the door*]. Oh goodness, I did!

GIOSETTA. Did you get me the bread?

GRAZIA [*returning*].   I did, I did!

ROBERTO. Would you say there's anything else you've forgotten?

GRAZIA. I haven't said good-morning to Roberto.

ROBERTO. It's just as well. I'm only half human as yet.

GRAZIA. Here's half a kiss, then, for the human part.

GIOSETTA. What have you been doing all this time?

GRAZIA. Watching the preparations down in the square.
  They've laid the sand for the race-track. Now the stalls
  And the seats are going up. And I've seen our horse!

[10]

It's right he should be called Midnight Pride,
He shines like a black star. Some flags are flying,
And they've begun draping the balconies.
Everyone I spoke to was a shade off balance
As though he had decided to go up in a balloon.
It was terribly hard to come away
And I forgot all about what I'd promised to do.
I'll get the things now.

ANGELINO [*going into the Palazzo*]. No matter, little pony.
I've taken them already.

GRAZIA [*starting to follow*]. Oh, thank you.

ALFIO [*to* LUIGI].   Excuse me, sir.

LUIGI. You know, we're the only two, Grazia,
Who seem to recognize what today stands for.
The happy times are coming out of their shelter.
They'll be a bit pale at first until the light
Gets to the skin; but there's a taste in the air
Of what it was like when we were boys, in a way.

GRAZIA. Is that what it is?

ROBERTO.   So he likes to imagine.

ALFIO [*to* ROBERTO]. Excuse me.

ROBERTO.   Quite all right.—But please God, it's not,
When you think of what that time was breeding.

GIOSETTA.   Grazia,
Who is this boy who came with you?

GRAZIA.   I don't know.
He was asking the way. He said he wanted to get here
So I brought him.

> [*She goes in through the big door. Exit* GIOSETTA *to apartment.*

[11]

LUIGI [*to* ALFIO].   Are you looking for someone?

ALFIO.   Yes,
Yes, I am. I wonder if you can tell me—

LUIGI. Now *you're* an impartial observer. Suppose you judge
The issue between my brother and me.
Is a man never to be allowed to grow
Out of the compost of his own mistakes
And be accepted on his present showing?
What good is served by treading ancient ordure
Into a new carpet? Kindly give us
Your oracular opinion.

ALFIO.   I was wanting to ask—

ROBERTO. You haven't convinced me that anything has altered.
You seem to think every change of wind
That crosses your mind is a kind of baptism.
Why don't you ask this chap what he's looking for?

LUIGI. He doesn't seem to have a thought in his head.
All right, what's he looking for?

ALFIO.   Someone who can give me
News of my father.

LUIGI.   I've never heard of him.

ROBERTO. Who *are* you if we had?

ALFIO.   I'm a jockey from Naples.
The Dragon district have hired me to ride for them.

LUIGI. Then, if I were you, I'd give this part of the town
A wide berth. Wouldn't you, Roberto?
I wouldn't take the responsibility
Of seeing you through these streets
Once it got about who you are. The Dragons
Are our oldest rivals. I'm not at all sure
It's not our duty to kidnap him. What do you think?

[12]

ROBERTO. I don't see that we've any alternative.

ALFIO [*backing away*]. Be serious, will you? I want some help.

LUIGI.   He thinks
We're not serious. Don't you know, Neapolitan numskull,
The race is more serious than matrimony.
Many's the wife goes home to her own district:
My wife, for instance—gone home to her mother
In a desperate state of divided loyalty.

ROBERTO. So you see there's no doubt we should quietly get rid
   of you.
What's your father to *us*?

ALFIO.   I don't know,
But I met a man very early in the war
Who said my father lives here, or at any rate
Lived here then. I've kept the address he gave me:
I'm afraid it's worn a bit thin down where the folds are,
But you see: Palazzo Traguardo, Via delle Stazioni.

ROBERTO. Right address.

ALFIO.   If I'd known the young woman lived here—

ROBERTO. But no redundant fathers.

LUIGI.   Unless—I say,
What about it, Roberto? What has daddo
Been doing while you and I were struggling to learn
To read and write?

ROBERTO.   Very funny!

LUIGI.   Eh? Why not?
Suppose we have here our little brother!
                              [*He shouts up to the Palazzo.*
                              DAD-DO!

ROBERTO. Stop it! You've irritated him once already.

[13]

LUIGI. What's your name, brother?

ALFIO.   Alfio Scapare.

ROBERTO. Scapare!

LUIGI [*after a pause*]. Aie! aie! aie!

ROBERTO.   Is your father
  Cesare Scapare?

ALFIO.   Yes. Is he living here?

ROBERTO. Not now.

ALFIO.   Where has he gone? Do you know?

LUIGI. Look, I think you'd better talk to my father.
  [*Shouts.*] Dad-do!—He'll tell you.

ALFIO.   What do you find so difficult?
  You don't have to mind telling me the truth.
  Is he dead?

                              [ANGELINO *looks out of a window.*

ANGELINO.   Were you calling me?

LUIGI.   We've someone here
  Who says he's Cesare Scapare's son.

ROBERTO. Don't let all the street hear you.

LUIGI [*to his father*].   So we thought
  You should come and talk to him.

ROBERTO [*to* ALFIO].   We can't tell you
  Whether he's dead or not.

              [ANGELINO *stares down at* ALFIO *without speaking. He
              withdraws from the window.* GIOSETTA *comes out and
              regards* ALFIO. *As* ANGELINO *comes into the courtyard
              she goes indoors.*

ALFIO. Why did your father look at me so strangely?

LUIGI. How else would he look at a stranger?

[14]

ALFIO.   I don't know,
But, between you, you've made me as jumpy as a cat.
What's the matter with all of you? Wasn't I asking
A simple enough question?

ROBERTO.   It's the simple questions
That take the most answering.
What you *should* know is, he has another family here—
A woman not your mother—a woman known
In these parts as his wife.

> [ANGELINO *enters.* GRAZIA *can be seen at the window
> looking at* ALFIO.

ANGELINO.   I thought the storm last night
Would open up a crack in the fabric somewhere.

LUIGI. This is Alfio Scapare.

ANGELINO.   And it has, sure enough.

ALFIO. Good-morning.

LUIGI.   He comes from Naples. And I'd say
He made a name for himself riding winners
When the war rolled on up north. At any rate
The Dragons have got him for their jockey.

ANGELINO. Quiet! You don't want that to get about
In this part of the town. He'll be in trouble.

LUIGI. We've told him that.

ALFIO.   Surely no one can object
To a man looking for his father?

ANGELINO.   Though, of course,
With the greatest respect, you're no threat to us at all;
We don't have to worry about *you*. We've got Cambriccio.
By some extraordinary stroke of luck—
Really we don't know how it came about—

[15]

We've got Cambriccio—and Cambriccio
As every living baby knows
Is an immortal centaur of a man.
Listen, he can lift a mare between his knees
And make her forget the ground weighs anything at all
Until he drops her at the post
Three lengths ahead of the field.
His riding is like holy love in a world
Given over to bed-bouncing. Don't imagine
I'm trying to undermine your confidence.
You may say you've got youth on your side, but, sweet jakes,
What's youth to genius?

ALFIO.   What about my father?

ANGELINO. No man in his senses would want to talk about
Your father when he can talk about Cambriccio.

ROBERTO. This man would. Tell him as much as we know.
Tell him why we feel guilty when he's mentioned.

ALFIO. I think you'd better.

ANGELINO.   Cesare Scapare,
You say he's your father. Well, well.
Yes, he lived here. You were shown the way
By his daughter.

LUIGI.   Your half-sister, you might say.

ALFIO. My sister?

LUIGI.   According to you.

ROBERTO.   Come on, it's time
We stopped dancing all round the ring. The history
Of your father, up to the time we lost him,
Is simply this: in nineteen forty-three
He was in the 'M' division at Bracciano.
And from there he deserted and made his way back home.

ALFIO. I have a half-sister?

ROBERTO.   Are you listening?

ALFIO. It's odd, isn't it, that I should have asked the way
  From her, of all people?

LUIGI.   My brother is taking
  A lot of painful trouble to answer your question.
  If you want to know, sit down, and keep your mind on it.

ALFIO. I'm sorry. Go on.

ROBERTO.   Did you hear me say he deserted?
  No sin. It was virtuous then to be a rat.
  Besides, Giosetta was ill. (You saw her just now,
  Grazia's mother.) There was no man to be got
  To work their olive-grove, and that was the whole
  Of their livelihood. My father lent a hand
  Whenever he could. But it was Grazia—
  She was only sixteen—who was cook and nurse,
  Housekeeper and labourer, getting no sleep
  Till she fell into it. So Cesare made for home.
  They hid him in the house during the day;
  At night he went out and worked among the olives.

ALFIO. And what then? What happened? They caught him, did
  they?

ROBERTO [*his eyes resting on* LUIGI].
  They did. Some Fascist big-mouth among us betrayed him.

ALFIO. Did they shoot him?

ROBERTO.   He sank out of sight; we know nothing
  More than that.

ANGELINO.   It was when he was leaving the house
  Late one night to go up into the fields.
  It was a night like the bottom of a pit, no moon.
  I was asleep, but I woke to hear

[17]

Cesare shout, three slams, and a jeep move off.
Then nothing, the bloody night sitting on my head
For a long minute, until Giosetta came
Crying across to me.

ROBERTO.   Now you can see why
We smile here with a gap in our front teeth.

[*A pause.*

ALFIO. I'd give something to know who gave him away. Who
   was it?
   Have you any suspicion?

ANGELINO.   Suspicion? Suspicion
   Was like a local sirocco blowing grit
   Into all our eyes, until even saints would look shifty.

ALFIO. What was he like, my father?
   I mean, how did he speak? How did he walk?
   Can you see anything of him in me?

ANGELINO.   Can we,
   Roberto? What do you think?

ROBERTO.   Stand up. Walk.

LUIGI. Grow two inches taller.

ANGELINO.   Something, perhaps,
   In the way he's been slung together. Eh? A kind
   Of falling back on an old design
   For want of a new basic principle.
   I wouldn't say more.

ALFIO.   Did you like him?

ANGELINO.   Cesare? Yes,
   Yes, he was one of the family here. Oh yes,
   I liked him. Three weeks out of the four
   You could get on well with him, and then for a bit
   He would drink himself into a puppet-man.

[18]

But never an explanation of what was grilling him—
As though he stuck his own legs in the stocks
And was hitting himself on the eyes with cabbage stalks.
You don't have to mourn over a lost hero, son.
It doesn't seem he gave much thought to you
Over the years.

> [GIOSETTA *has come out of her door. She turns sharply on* ANGELINO. *As the speech goes on she occasionally gives a rug a whack with a stick.*

GIOSETTA.   How do you know what he thought?
Does a man have to flay the skin off his body
And hang it on your door, you old leather-merchant,
Before you can speak any good of him? Don't imagine
That Cesare kept his boy a secret from me,
I know all about him. Fancy, Angelino Bruno
Judging his neighbours! We can very soon
Have the three black gypsies you call sons
Put up on show, the way you've done to Cesare.
Let me just tell you.
This fine judge of men you see here, Alfio,
Said to his boys as each one came to leave school:
'I've saved a poor man's fortune from the leather shop
And I'll set you up in any profession you name.'

ANGELINO. Giosetta!

GIOSETTA.   That one, hefting his eyebrow at me,
Roberto, he said he would be a doctor,
And as far as it goes I suppose he is a doctor,
But his real ambition is to see us all
Peppered with bullets at the barricades
And carried off on stretchers to the casualty station.

> [LUIGI *laughs.*

GIOSETTA. As for this one, Luigi, he was to be the politician.
He has the biggest mouth in the family.
No other profession could keep it in the style
It was used to—but all that's come of it
Is reporting football matches in the local paper
As though they were grand opera.

ANGELINO. Now, now, Giosetta, don't let's have any more—

GIOSETTA. As for the other one, the third bright product,
The one that we're not allowed to mention—

                      [ANGELINO *groans and sits down.*

GIOSETTA. He looked straight into his father's eyes and said
'Give me enough to get going and I promise
I'll be as good a thief as any in the business.
That's my ambition, I want to be a thief.'
Well, at least he knew where his talents lay
Which is more than can be said of his brothers.
But poor Angelino, he couldn't understand
Such honest self-appreciation.
So the boy went straight off to Giovanni Levanti
Who worked in the shop in those days, and borrowed
The whole of his savings. That was his word for it: 'borrowed'.
He knew something about Giovanni and didn't
Leave him any choice, and then departed the country.
He started off as he meant to go on. That's all
About him. Now you know what family it is
That doesn't know how to speak well of Cesare.

ANGELINO. Do you mean we still exist? What have I said
To deserve such a terrible beating, Giosetta?
I was only trying to ease the boy's mind, and you've made
All my old wounds ache.

ALFIO.   Please excuse me;
I didn't know I was going to cause so much trouble.

[20]

LUIGI. You'll see how well we survive. Her curse is never
Altogether fatal. We still limp on.
        [GIOSETTA *blows her nose and wipes away the tears of*
        excitement.

GIOSETTA. You dare to be hurt by what I say, Angelino!
You've sinned quite enough making me angry,
Don't sin worse by making me sorry I was,
Don't you dare.

ROBERTO.   Giovanni Levanti died
Last night, Giosetta.

GIOSETTA [*crossing herself*]. Rest his soul. I guessed
It would come. He was smelling the ground all this last year.
I hope the next world enjoys him as much as we did.
Let's be friends, Angelino.

ANGELINO.   Well, I should think so.
                [*She kisses him and goes on to kiss* ROBERTO.

GIOSETTA. What a morning it is.

ROBERTO [*kissing her*].   Every minute of it.

LUIGI. Here's someone else needs your attention, Giosetta.
Make me well again.

GIOSETTA.   I don't take back a word.
I've told you what I think—[*kiss*]—and there's
Confirmation of it.

LUIGI.   Giosetta loves us.
        [GIOSETTA *turns rather shyly to* ALFIO. GRAZIA *is standing*
        in the great doorway.

GIOSETTA. Cesare's boy. What do we say to each other?

ALFIO. Words are like dynamite here. Is it safe to apologize?

GIOSETTA [*approaching to kiss him*]. Why? Because you happen to
live?

ALFIO [*kissed*].   Thank you.
        [GIOSETTA *turns away and comes face to face with* GRAZIA.

GRAZIA. Yes, I've heard all about it, and I think it might
    Have been better if I'd heard it before; but I'm too
    Young for truth, I suppose. And yet, you see,
    I brought it here. Good-morning, truth.

ALFIO.   Good-morning.

GIOSETTA. I wanted to tell you, Grazia.

GRAZIA.   It doesn't matter.
        [*There is a clatter of churns out in the street and a shout of
        'Water!'* A MAN (FRANCO) *trundles in a metal churn,
        followed by a* SECOND MAN *with another churn.*

ROBERTO. Thank God for that.

ANGELINO.   In plenty of time
    For the travellers. Over there, that's it, Franco.
                [FRANCO *trundles the churn towards the great door.*

ROBERTO. Here, wait a minute! Wait a minute, now.
    How many churns are you leaving, Franco?

FRANCO [*looking at his paper*].   Let's see.
    Palazzo del Traguardo. . . . Two families.
    Two churns.

ROBERTO.   It's not enough. The Palazzo
    Is going to be lived in. We shall have to have three.

FRANCO. Here's nothing about that, comrade. Two churns.

ROBERTO. Then we'll have it over here.

ANGELINO.   Oh, no, we won't.
    No, no, this must be for the Palazzo.
    What a welcome, to find no water when they arrive!
                [*The* SECOND MAN *has taken a churn to* GIOSETTA.

[22]

SECOND MAN. Sign here, please.

[GIOSETTA *signs and goes indoors.*

ANGELINO. Roberto, just think, will you?
Coming from wherever they've come from, getting here
With dust and sweat silting up their navels,
And then to be told there's no water in the house.
I'd never get over it. I'll let you take
Enough to shave your obstinate jaw-line, and that's
As much as you're going to have, my son.

[ROBERTO *sits on the churn.*

ROBERTO. Generous,
But as you see, I'm establishing squatter's rights.

ANGELINO. Get off there!

ROBERTO. We don't yield a drop to the enemy.

FRANCO. Sign, comrade. Make up your own minds.

ALFIO. Grazia.

GRAZIA. What is it?

ALFIO. Can you spare a moment?

GRAZIA. I don't know that I can. What do you want to say?

ROBERTO [*to* FRANCO]. Keep going, Aquarius.

FRANCO. What's that?

ROBERTO. Ciao, comrade.

FRANCO. Ciao.

ANGELINO [*following him into the street*].
Can you come back with another delivery?
This is very important. . . . You go and tell them at the office. . . .

ALFIO. Are you minding this, Grazia, having a brother?

GRAZIA. I am, for the time being. I feel jostled.

ALFIO. When I came up to you to ask you the way
You were as friendly as the first sun of the year

[23]

On the back of my neck. Now that I'm your brother
You can't wait to be rid of me.

GRAZIA.   Yes, I can; I can wait.
                  [ROBERTO *trundles the churn towards the Osteria.*

ROBERTO [*to* LUIGI]. Round one. Ahead on points.

LUIGI. Don't drop your guard, not for a second, Bobo.
   They'll nip in with a staggering right, when you least expect it.

ALFIO [*to* GRAZIA]. When the race is over I shall go back to
   Naples.
   You don't have to put up with me for long.
   What's wrong with half a brother for less than a week?

GRAZIA. It's not so much that. But now I have to think
   Of a double father, yours and mine.

ALFIO.   Dear God,
   I'd like to find the man who betrayed him.

GRAZIA [*sharply*].   Don't say it!

ALFIO. I'd make him feel sorry. If it were possible
   I wouldn't go back to Naples till I've dug him out.

GRAZIA. Then I don't want to see you again! You're like
   A dog scratching for an old bone
   With mud plastered on your snout
   And your paws going like a piston. I hate it!
   I can't stand here talking to you.
   I've got better things to do.

                       [*She moves swiftly away.*

ALFIO.   Now what's the matter?
   Why shouldn't I want to know who did it?
   What's so wrong about that?

GRAZIA.   Oh, go away,
   Be quiet! I've had more than enough of you!

                       [*She goes into the house.*

[24]

ALFIO. Well, that seems to be the end of my experience
  As a brother.

LUIGI.   What do you mean, the end?
  You're one of the family now. It's only beginning.

ALFIO. I feel safer on my Vespa.
        [ANGELINO *returns from the street and finds that* ROBERTO
        has moved the churn into the Osteria.

ANGELINO.   What has he done with it?
  Roberto, bring it back here! Roberto!
  Listen to me, this is very serious,
  You're giving me the guts' ache, where's your consideration
  For other people, eh? Bring it back and behave
  Like a dear good son, you thieving scoundrel.
  I won't forgive you if you don't let me have it.
  What about equal rights and opportunities?

ROBERTO'S VOICE. That makes it ours for certain!

ANGELINO.   You're making me cry!
        [*He has followed* ROBERTO *in through the door and his
        voice disappears into the recesses of the house.*

LUIGI [*laughing*]. As a family we're so close
  You only have to breathe and you hear a rib crack.

ALFIO. I'd better go and find a quiet corner
  Where I can pat my nerves down, otherwise
  I shall electrocute my horse at the practice run
  This afternoon. How do you all do it?
  My shirt's like a hot compress.

LUIGI.   Very warm,
  Very warm.
                        [GRAZIA *looks out of a window.*

GRAZIA.   Alfio, I wanted to say
  I'm sorry I flew at you.

B   [25]

ALFIO.   That's all right.
I'm just going, Grazia. Do you think we could—Oh.

[GRAZIA *has left the window.*

ANGELINO *enters.*

ANGELINO. You must help me, Luigi! What am I going to do?
He's threatening to pour it all into the bath
And get into it if I say any more.

LUIGI.   You know
He won't listen to me, daddo.

ANGELINO.   Why does he do it?
Why does he want to ruin me? What a chance
Will be gone for you, too, Luigi! Think of it!
Offending people of such influence and wealth
As they're sure to be. They might have taken
A great interest in you, if we'd treated them well.
What a brother!

LUIGI.   Come on. It won't do any good,
But come on!

[*They go into the Osteria.* ALFIO *has thought of going to
find* GRAZIA *but has thought better of it and lights a
cigarette.* GIOSETTA *has entered in time to hear* ANGELINO'S
distress.

GIOSETTA.   The Brunos can make an ant-hill erupt.
It's just as well some of us keep steady heads.
Hold this, Alfio. I don't want the whole reservoir.
We'll fill these bowls, and you can take the rest
Across for the big nobs. Will you do that?
Then I'll put some coffee on; we can talk to each other.

[*They set about filling two large bowls and a jug.*

ALFIO. Isn't it natural I should want to find out
Who it was betrayed him? Grazia was against it,
But he is my father.

[26]

GIOSETTA.   The night they came for him
Isn't half an hour old yet for you. But we
Have borne it nearly three years, and I can't stand
Any more anger being here instead of Cesare.
Neither can Grazia, I dare say. After a time
You have to want to look at people again.
You have to wake in the morning, without the light
Pushing you back down on the mattress.
I weigh a stone and a half more than I did,
And hope to increase when the warm weather's over.
          [*She takes a bowl indoors and comes back to take the second
          bowl from* ALFIO.

GIOSETTA. Did you ever ask your mother about him?

ALFIO.   Of course.
But she might have been talking about some Roman emperor.
I doubt if they ever met. She's ill, and has been
As long as I remember. We need the money
I make on this race, though it won't do much.

GIOSETTA. Come back and talk about her.
          [*She goes back indoors while* ALFIO *trundles the churn
          across the yard to the great door. At the same time* LUIGI
          *emerges from the Osteria trundling the other churn. He is
          followed by* ROBERTO, *naked except for a towel, his chin
          lathered with shaving-soap, and bare-footed. Close behind
          him comes* ANGELINO.

ROBERTO. You'll hand that over, Luigi. This is no
Business of yours.

ANGELINO.   He's my representative,
I told him to deal with you.

ROBERTO.   That's it: now
Cheat me of my birthright, give your blessing

[27]

To the hairless-chested junior. I don't accept it!
This goes with me.

LUIGI.   I'm standing up for the rights
Of an alien minority.

ROBERTO.   You're interfering
In our domestic politics. Give up
Or you'll get hurt!

LUIGI.   You can't terrorize us.
Get back to your mountains.

                    [ROBERTO *loses his temper and attacks* LUIGI.

ANGELINO.   Stop it, Roberto,
You're a grown man! You've got a medical degree!
No, no, really, we've got things to do.

                    [*He is alarmed by the ferocity of* ROBERTO'*s attack and
                    tries to intervene.*

For pity's sake, Roberto, what are you doing?
What's got into you?

LUIGI [*frightened*].   Do you want to kill me?
                    [*A beautiful woman,* ANA-CLARA, *enters through the arch.
                    She wears a simple dress with one handsome brooch of
                    diamonds. At this moment* ROBERTO *slings* LUIGI *against
                    the wall;* LUIGI *slides to the ground.* ANGELINO *collapses
                    on to a chair.*

ROBERTO. Be more careful what you say.

LUIGI.   Be careful yourself!

ROBERTO. You don't know what you do to me.

LUIGI.   What I
Do to *you*!

ANGELINO. What I have to live with!

ROBERTO. Understood, the Nabobs have no claim on the water.

[28]

ANA-CLARA. Is this the Palazzo del Traguardo?

ANGELINO [*leaping to his feet*].   Dear lady!
 I didn't see you.

ANA-CLARA.   It's not to be wondered at.
    [ROBERTO *is embarrassed by his state of undress, his face
    smeared with dried lather, and still shaken by what has hap-
    pened. He thinks of making a bolt for cover, but decides to
    remain.* LUIGI *laughs.* ROBERTO *takes a squashed packet
    from* LUIGI's *shirt pocket and helps himself to a cigarette.*

ANA-CLARA. Perhaps, before the naked arm of authority—
 The handsome naked arm of authority—
 Throws me down, too, for common trespass,
 I should tell you my business is, in the first degree,
 Lawful. This is the Palazzo del Traguardo?

ANGELINO. Yes, it is, Signora. I apologize,
 My sons felt they must bring a difference
 Into the open.

ANA-CLARA [*looking round her*]. What does the foreground matter?
 Here's the attraction. Built in fifteen ninety-two.

ANGELINO. Quite right, Signora; the architect—

ANA-CLARA.   Bernardo
 Buontalenti. You see I have brought my credentials.
 And you are Angelino Bruno, born
 At San Gimignano in eighteen ninety-three,
 Three hundred years the junior. I'm happy to meet you.
 You were expecting me, or I hope you were.

ANGELINO. Indeed, of course: we were all expectant,
 And everything was in order, everything
 Ship-shape to receive you: only, last night
 A most untimely cloudburst—and which of us
 Can hope to discipline the storm?—

Confused the water and the sewage system,
And, of course, the Commune, alert to the dangers
Of epidemic, turned off the storm-cock,
Not the storm-cock, I mean the stop-cock,
The result is a breakdown in the water supply.

ROBERTO. And a shakiness in other communications,
As you can hear. My father is upset
Because the Palazzo is without any water.
Which, I'm afraid, I'm answerable for.
The main supply is cut, and no provision
Was made for any to be brought for you.
In my father's view, which I've been obstructing,
You should be given ours.

ANA-CLARA.   But of course
A dust-bath is all I need.

ANGELINO.   No question who has it.
You mustn't take this son of mine seriously.

ANA-CLARA. I think I may have to.

                    [LUIGI *has noticed* GIOSETTA's *churn.*

LUIGI.   Who put this here?

ALFIO. I did. Grazia's mother didn't need it all.

ROBERTO. Treachery!

ANGELINO.   That's a good thing. Then our worries are
    over.

ANA-CLARA [*to* ROBERTO]. Are you the black sheep of the family?

LUIGI. No, madam, he's the red sheep. We have
A black sheep, but he isn't with us.

ROBERTO. If you'll excuse me, I'll put some clothes on.
It may spoil your fantasy of coming to live
Among the barefooted tribe of the poor, but it's better

[30]

You shouldn't expect more romance than we can give you.
Excuse me.

[He goes into the Osteria.

ANGELINO.   Well, you will want to see the Palazzo.

ANA-CLARA.   I embarrassed him. Now he will never like me.
As for the Palazzo, I had to promise
Not even to peer in through a window until
My husband gets here. May we sit and talk,
And feel less like strangers in a railway carriage?

LUIGI.   May I fetch you a drink?

ANA-CLARA.   No, thank you.—I'm in disgrace
With my husband, too. His eyebrows ran down his nose—
A bad omen always—when I told him I meant
To arrive without him. A man can't understand
Women prefer to spin a home,
Out of the belly like a spider,
Not be laid in it like a cuckoo's egg.
So I walked all the way, a willing novice
Learning her neighbourhood. Each façade
And little piazza, shop doorway and swag of washing
Instructed me into my different life.
You see how brilliantly your son diagnosed
The romantic in me.

ANGELINO.   Roberto is a doctor.

ANA-CLARA.   I believe it; he makes an incision with his eye.

LUIGI.   You're not Italian. Is it Spain? Where do you come from?

ANA-CLARA.   I'm Portuguese.

LUIGI.   I see; and could you tell me
Is it just by chance that you arrive this week,
The week of the Palio—the sensational week
When the city celebrates an immortal identity,

[31]

When it hymns our power of survival over oppression,
Defeat and death?

ANA-CLARA.　　　　Not in the least by chance.
It has been my—do you say, lodestar?

LUIGI.　　　　　　　　　　　Wonderful!
Then you understand how significant this year's race is,
The first since the war. You know how it all began?
Four centuries ago, or nearly that,
The city held out through a siege for months
Until the skeleton third of the population,
All that was left, pushed open the gates
And let the enemy in.
The parish companies were stripped of their arms
But were 'armed in the spirit', so history says.
Instead of being military defenders
They became civil protectors of our liberties
And the city straightened its vertebrae to a ramrod.
And that's what we celebrate in the Palio:
Pride in our flair for resurrection,
Excitement, violence and rivalry,
With the Mother of God as carnival queen.
Spare a lira for the guide, lady.

ANA-CLARA. He's worth a hundred.

　　　　　　　　　　　[*She kisses his outstretched palm.*
　　　　　　　　　　　Like the poet's blind

Tiresias, I have seen it all.

LUIGI.　　　　　　You've seen it?

ANA-CLARA. As an article of faith. Whenever I closed
My eyes on hot afternoons in Portugal.
I heard it so often described, never enough
To match my curiosity. I persevered
With endless questions, to trap the forgotten detail,

[32]

Until I could set it all in train by drowsing.
What I fancied I saw was common life,
Particularly the common male, glorified!
Striped, pied, blazoned and crested,
Pausing and advancing like courting sunbirds—
Indeed, the whole deliberate procession
Like an unhurried lovemaking. Isn't it so?
The first shock of the gun, and the trumpets
That stop the heart, until it beats again
With the rap of the kettle-drums, and the pouring in
Of colour on the pale square. The huge voice
Of the crowd is like the roar of blood in the ears.
The Commune flag fluttering, while the Commune bell
Jerks in the erect campanile,
Like an alarm, and like a gloria; both.
And all the time the banners ripple and leap,
Circle the body, stroke and rouse
With creating hands. Oh, it really is, you know,
A lovemaking, a fishing in sensitive pools.

LUIGI [*undoing his tie and collar*].
Excuse me; today's going to be a lion,
And it's only ten o'clock.—You won't make me
Believe you were never here, I won't have that.

ANA-CLARA. At last when the corporate body has been tautened
Absolutely to expectation's limit
There comes the violent release, the orgasm,
The animal explosion of the horse race,
Bare-backed and savage. After that—well, after that
I am lost in the dispersing crowd, I give way
To my siesta.

LUIGI.   Confess you have seen it.

[33]

ANA-CLARA. No, I promise. I have only lived it,
Not seen it. But I shall, now, after all.
What are our chances?—yours, I mean. What price
The Pelican? Have we any hope on earth?
What horse, what rider?

> [ANGELINO *is open-mouthed, totally absorbed in* ANA-CLARA. *He has to pull himself together.*

ANGELINO. Eh? The horse? He's a hero, a black-veined hero.
But what's remarkable for us, what's really remarkable
Is to have Cambriccio to ride him, the greatest
In the land. And the mystery is how we came by him!
He's been hired at God knows what cost by no one.

ANA-CLARA. No one?

ANGELINO.   A nameless one, a blessed unknowable
power
Who loves us. We can be as sure we shall win
As we are of tomorrow's light. The entire parish
Have put their savings on it, and sleep dreamless
On their backs the whole night through.

ANA-CLARA.   A lamblike faith
In life's justice.

LUIGI.   But this is a certainty!

> [ALFIO *enters from* GIOSETTA'S *apartment. He calls across
> to* ANGELINO *and* LUIGI.

ALFIO. Goodbye, then!

ANGELINO.   You going?

LUIGI.   Try to keep out of trouble.
Sorry you fared so badly with us. Did you
Have any better luck?

> GRAZIA *enters from the great door.*

[34]

ALFIO.   Well, I. . . . What
Do you call luck? Yes, I suppose so. Goodbye.
> [GRAZIA *crosses to him and kisses him on both cheeks.*

GRAZIA. There, that's the best I can do.

ALFIO.   Good enough.
Thanks very much. Ciao.

LUIGI.   Don't imagine
You're going to win on that horse of yours.
> [ALFIO *laughs, picks up his Vespa and wheels it into the road.*
> LUIGI *turns to* ANA-CLARA.

LUIGI. He's the boy who's riding for the enemy parish,
Our deadly rivals. Don't ask what brought him here.
It made the pebbles hop.

ANGELINO.   Never mind about that.
Come along, Grazia, come and be introduced.
We all depend in the end on Grazia.
This is Grazia Scapare. I'm sorry to say
I haven't been told your name, I must apologize—
> [ALFIO *has started up the Vespa and rides away.*

ANA-CLARA. Who is it, did you say? I couldn't hear you.

ANGELINO. GRAZIA SCAPARE!

ANA-CLARA.   I am happy to meet you.
> [*As* ANA-CLARA *takes* GRAZIA'S *hand there is a screech of
> brakes and the blare of a klaxon.*

LUIGI. Mother of God!

ANGELINO.   What has happened?

GRAZIA [*covering her eyes*].   No accident, please!

LUIGI. He's all right, I think. He's gone swerving on down the
road.
Two cars: one just kissed the backside of the other.
No harm done.

[35]

ANGELINO. Do you think this might be your husband?

ANA-CLARA. If he almost drove over someone, I think it might be. If he drove right over them, yes, it is my husband.

GRAZIA. They're unloading the luggage.

ANGELINO. They don't need help?

LUIGI. No, they don't need help.

ANGELINO [*to* ANA-CLARA]. So now your patience
Can be rewarded, Signora. But remember,
Do bear in mind, the Palazzo's been occupied
By the military, used for billeting
The Germans and then the Americans, but only
The higher ranks, who knew the value of things
(You will find certain things are missing): although
We had one sorry adventure when a Colonel
Put several bullets through his own reflection
In a gilded mirror two centuries old. They say
He had seen himself once too often. And less than a week
Later he was blown up in his car. If only
He could have faced what he was five days longer!
We could put in some new glass, unless you think
It should be left as a minor historical
Souvenir.

ANA-CLARA. You mustn't be so nervous.
No one ever sold my husband what he didn't want.

LUIGI. Here come the troops.

> [*Enter a* MANSERVANT *carrying luggage, followed by one or two more, a* SECRETARY, *a* LADY'S MAID, *and a* CHAUFFEUR *carrying hand-luggage.* ANGELINO *takes the first* MANSERVANT *to the main door, and turns in astonishment to see the rest of the retinue.*

[36]

ANGELINO. Ah, yes. Good-morning. This is the way. If you would take it through here. Can you see where to go? It's a little dark at first after the light outside. Good gracious. Yes, I see. Good-morning. Just follow your... all right? Good-morning. Well, it's quite a load. A good thing we got the rain over last night. Oh, excuse me—more. Is that everything, then?

> [*Meanwhile* LUIGI *is talking to* ANA-CLARA.

LUIGI. Am I going to like your husband?

ANA-CLARA.   We shall see.
   Is it in his favour to say that I do, or will you
   Hold that against him?

LUIGI.   I haven't quite decided.
   Is he at all interested in politics?

ANA-CLARA. Where they affect his interests; of course.

LUIGI. He may want to know more about the parties here,
   In Italy.

ANA-CLARA. It's possible.

LUIGI.   I could help him in that.

> [GRAZIA *has gone indoors. Now she returns with* GIOSETTA.
> *Into the archway enters a young man,* ANA-CLARA'*s hus-*
> *band. His wealth is subtly stressed in his clothes.* LUIGI
> *suddenly sees him.*

LUIGI. My God! Daddo, look here! Excuse
   My language, but here's Edmondo, Edmondo!

> [*He bursts out laughing.* EDMONDO *stands grinning.*
> ANGELINO *disengages himself from the servants in be-*
> *wilderment.*

ANGELINO. What? What do you say? On my living soul—
   Edmondo!

EDMONDO.   That's who it is.

ANGELINO.   But does this mean
   You came with the gentleman, too?

DMONDO.   If you put it like that.
I am the gentleman.
                          [ANGELINO *looks dazedly towards* ANA-CLARA.

ANGELINO.   This lady's . . . ?

ANA-CLARA.   Husband.
He's quite right.

LUIGI [*to* ANA-CLARA]. You've had some fun with us.

ANGELINO. My son Edmondo!

EDMONDO.   Daddo!

ANGELINO.   My son Edmondo,
My dear son!

GIOSETTA.   He's off the Index for good.
                          [ANGELINO *embraces and kisses* EDMONDO *on both cheeks.*
                          LUIGI *shouts into the Osteria.*

LUIGI. Roberto! Come out and meet the enemy.
You've missed the great moment, you poor man.
You're needed on the reception committee.

EDMONDO. I thought I'd surprise you. The surprise of your life
Isn't it?

LUIGI [*embracing him*]. You great, crafty, secretive,
Successful squit, welcome home.

EDMONDO.   You old orator!
Why haven't you got your feet up in the Quirinale?

LUIGI. How do you know I haven't?

ANGELINO.   Remember the Scapares?
I've had astonishing dreams, but never so wild
As this.

EDMONDO. Do I remember them? Where's his mind gone?

GIOSETTA. You've done your best to shatter it.

[38]

EDMONDO.   Dear Giosetta.
But what about this, eh? What magician
Has been busy here? Don't tell me this is Grazia!
Time changes us all, but here's a miracle.

GRAZIA. Hullo.

EDMONDO.   Hullo? Is that all I get?

LUIGI.   Edmondo,
Come to the climax. We know you own the earth;
What about your shares in some other heavenly body?
Present us to the lady. Until you do
I won't believe she belongs to a brother
Whose cold feet I once shared a bed with.

ANA-CLARA. I'm out of favour.

EDMONDO.   You've already met her.
That was her own idea. She wouldn't wait
To be the culmination, the way I planned for her.

ANA-CLARA. Imagine what he wanted! I crouch in the car
Till the whip cracks, and the brass brays,
And in I shuffle, mad, in hot spangles.
Haven't we done better than that, father-in-law?

                            [*She kisses* ANGELINO.

ANGELINO. Foof! My heart's like a pile-driver. I've never
Gone up in the world so fast. What an outcome
To my life, after all!

EDMONDO.   Her name is Ana-Clara.
            [*Enter* ROBERTO. *He wears a clean shirt and a rather worn
            grey suit, and carries a doctor's bag.*

LUIGI. Here he is at last. How about this?

ROBERTO. God above, where did you turn up from?

EDMONDO. The authentic voice of my big brother, anyway.

[39]

LUIGI. Careful, my boy, he's the king of the castle,
   He's taken over the Palazzo.

ROBERTO [*with a hacking laugh*]. Is that true?
   You've brought off the best joke of your life, then.
   Congratulations. You should have seen the awful
   Preparations. We've been putting grease on our joints
   Ready to genuflect.

EDMONDO.   And so you should.
   Well, are you glad to see me?

ROBERTO.   Why shouldn't I be?
   I'm all for the substance, as a healthy change
   From the old taboo.

EDMONDO.   You haven't met him, Ana-Clara,
   The eldest of us?

ANA-CLARA.   Not this finished portrait;
   Only a bare outline. I am very pleased—

ROBERTO. To watch the peasant wince?

ANA-CLARA.   It was a compliment
   In anyone's language but yours.

LUIGI.   Tell us, Edmondo,
   How you have done it, where in the world you have been,
   Where have you come from?

EDMONDO.   Portugal.

ROBERTO.   Portugal?

ANGELINO. We can't have the story frittered away,
   That won't do; I want to savour it,
   Every blessed minute of the adventure
   Since you went out through the door. I'm starving for it,
   But I won't be fed with crumbs.

LUIGI [*ironically*].   We need excitement.
Nothing but a war ever happens
To us stay-at-homes.

EDMONDO.   I've got about the world,
I can say that. Starting in South America.

ROBERTO. What were you doing in Portugal?

EDMONDO.   Dad's right,
Let's keep the story until the evening, until
After he's gone to the cellar and brought us up
The best the old vineyard had to offer.

ANGELINO [*distressed*].   It's gone,
It's all gone, my dear child. And I cossetted it
And nursed it all those years, if for nothing else
For the breath of the old summers when you were boys
And mamma living. I promise you,
I took such care of it you couldn't tell us apart—
Not for this occasion, of course: *this* occasion
I couldn't have imagined—but for when things would prosper.
But when the Nazis started to pull out
They smashed the bottles, and riddled the barrels with bullets.
I'd almost rather it had been my own blood
That swamped the floor. What a tragedy!
This is when it hurts again. That wine would have made you
A great speech of welcome.

EDMONDO.   Well, don't let's have
Any tears—it wasn't the best in the world, anyway.

LUIGI. Never mind, we can give him the best horse and the best
Rider, can't we, daddo?

ANGELINO.   That's what we *can* do,
What a blessing! How well it all comes together.
Edmondo, you're going to see the race of your life:

Our horse coming home in front, snorting clouds
In your honour. You can smile if you like,
But I'll jail myself for fraud if we don't win.

EDMONDO. Oh, yes, we'll win. We had to make sure of it this time.

LUIGI. What do you mean? Who made sure?

EDMONDO.   I did.

ANGELINO. Are you saying it was you who hired Cambriccio?

EDMONDO. That's what I'm saying.

ANGELINO.   Every extraordinary thing
Turns into you. You got us Cambriccio?

EDMONDO. What? I couldn't leave such a thing to chance.
We're into the great festival week of the Brunos,
Nothing goes wrong, Edmondo's home; there isn't
Place for anything less than total pleasure,
Not in my organization of life, anyhow.

ANGELINO. Even Cambriccio!

GRAZIA [*suddenly*].   How could you bear the silence?

EDMONDO. Me? What silence?—You know, its remarkable!
I can't get over Grazia, a grown-up woman.
Thank God the skipping rope I brought her
Is made of pearls.

GRAZIA.   While you have been away:
That silence; not exchanging a word
Or trying to find out what was happening.
How did you live your day or sleep at night
When all the time you could have known something?
I don't understand, when worse news came after bad,
How you could trust anything, and simply plan
To come back as though nothing could have changed.

EDMONDO. I'm in the dock, am I?

ANGELINO.   The doctor said

[42]

When they'd got you off the umbilical hook
'*There's* a promising cranium.' The spirit
Of prophecy was in him, that's all I can think.

EDMONDO. I can tell her. You won't remember, Grazia,
But I wasn't popular when I left home—

ANGELINO. Mea culpa, mea culpa.

EDMONDO.   I don't blame anybody,
But I couldn't know what sort of a reception
A letter from me would get. So I thought I'd wait
Until I was sure of a welcome.

ANGELINO.   Mea culpa.
The pride and pleasure I've missed.

EDMONDO.   Stop moaning, daddo.
Anyway, I soon got on the right side of life.
It all worked like sap in a happy tree.
And the old war-god wasn't averse to me either
When I saw how to handle him. I say that because,
When things turned rough, it meant I had my spies,
Useful contacts in high places,
Who would give a preserving eye to my family.
Anxiety could be kept at a minimum.

                               [There is a general gasp at this.

LUIGI. I see now what has happened. He has taken
Over the world, that's it, of course it is!
How did you get along with my guardian angel,
Or was he too disillusioned to say anything?

ROBERTO. But it's not a joke. And a very long way from it.
Who *were* these sinister contacts he was coupling
Our name with? *Who* were these benefactors?
The Black Brigades? The S.S.? Or the genocides
Of Berlin? What circle of the inferno
Do we owe our preservation to?

ANA-CLARA [*her face in her hands*]. Oh, dear.

EDMONDO. Steady on. I was talking about business connections.
I'm an internationalist, the same as any
Reasonable business man. My interest
Is where the market is.
[*With a flash of anger.*] I must say *you*
Made it just about as difficult for me
As any man could!

ROBERTO.   Crucifixion! Made
It difficult! Hasn't one maggot
Of what's been happening crawled into your head?
Would it surprise you to know, we've not been tormented
By flies, but bloody torture of the spirit.
This land has fought and suffered, do you know what that means?
While you were piling up profits, however you did it.
                      [ANGELINO *has been whimpering to intervene.*

ANGELINO. Edmondo was doing his best to help us—how could he
Guess all the circumstances? I won't hear any more!

EDMONDO. I'm sorry, I apologize. That was a hark-back
To resisting the elder brother talk; I'm sorry.

LUIGI. You underestimated your effect, 'Mondo.
We're a local lot here; we have to get used to you.

GIOSETTA. Cesare was taken.
                      [*A pause.* EDMONDO *nods.*

EDMONDO.   Something went very wrong there.
                      [GRAZIA *suddenly goes into the house.*

ANA-CLARA. Let me say this: no man born could have talked
About you all with such relentless affection
As Edmondo did, until I could hear you breathe.
Even turn to the door expecting you to be there.
You were more real than the world I grew up in.

[44]

Any man can make a woman his wife,
But Edmondo made me daughter and sister, too,
As if I always had been, by the force of his memories.
From the day I first met him his guiding thought
Has been to come home with his arms crowded with blessings.
It became my purpose, too.

ANGELINO.   There has never been
A prouder day. To think of my own son
Master of the Palazzo, and bringing with him
Such a—

ANA-CLARA. Wife and daughter.

ANGELINO.   Sky-born lady.

EDMONDO. Well, you can all have the life you want now,
That's the point.

LUIGI.   Good old Edmondo, you can
Lead me by the hand anywhere you like.

EDMONDO. It's time we made our tour of inspection. See
If my memory slapped the gold on too thick, shall we?
There's never been a sky for me like the blue skies
Painted on the ceilings. I had pubic dreams
Of flying up and butting the pink nipples
Of the sprawling nudes with my little bullet head.

ANGELINO. The paint is flaking here and there.

EDMONDO.   We'll see to that.
Where's Grazia? There are presents to unwrap.
You'd better all come and stand in line.

GIOSETTA.   I'll find her.

                              [GIOSETTA *goes in.*

EDMONDO. How's Giovanni Levanti?

ROBERTO.   He died last night.

[45]

EDMONDO. Damn. Last night. Oh, damn. I'd brought him back
A small fortune, the fruits of his investment.
Only last night? Well, his son must have it.

LUIGI. Mario was killed.

EDMONDO.   Oh.

LUIGI.   There's just his daughter.

EDMONDO. That's right, then Rosa must have it. What a shame
I can't surprise him, though. I had it all planned. . . .
Pity. Now, where are the keys of the kingdom, daddo?

ANGELINO. All hanging here.

EDMONDO.   What a size, eh?
St. Peter must have a forearm. . . .

ROBERTO.   Look at the time.
I have calls to make.

          [CHAUFFEUR *and a* MANSERVANT *come out of the house.*

SERVANT. Excuse me, sir, the Mayor's office is on the telephone.

EDMONDO. Roberto, why don't you have the car, to drive you
Wherever you have to go? . . . Yes, you have it.

                              [LUIGI *laughs delightedly.*

ROBERTO. No, thanks, they would think I had come with the
hearse.

EDMONDO. Well, we shan't need you, then, Ettore,
Until, let's say four o'clock. All right, Luciano,
I'll come with you now.

          [*He goes in, followed by* ANGELINO. LUIGI *hesitates in the
          doorway.*

LUIGI.   What are you doing, Edmondo?—
[*To* ANA-CLARA]. The great moment of the ceremony,
Taking you over the threshold—and he forgets it!
Who is to do it: me?

ANA-CLARA.　　　　The ceremony
　Was already in shreds.

LUIGI.　　　　　　Oh, Bobo! He had no sleep.
　He's more than ordinarily sensitive
　To the shame of life this morning. I found that out.

ANA-CLARA. Go in, don't wait. I'll join you.

LUIGI.　　　　　　　　Right.
　　　　　　　　[*He darts into the Palazzo.*

ANA-CLARA. Do you always give dreams such a rough reception?

ROBERTO. If they call for it.

ANA-CLARA.　　　　I'm trying to imagine
　Your bedside manner.

ROBERTO.　　　　What was he doing in Portugal?

ANA-CLARA. He was making love to me. Does that disturb you?

ROBERTO. There's no mystery there. But what's his line of
　　business,
　How have all these profits piled up on his hands?

ANA-CLARA. Too much gold in his bloodstream, is that
　The symptom that worries you?

ROBERTO.　　　　　　Yes, it is
　When I think of his adolescent ailments.

ANA-CLARA.　　　　　　Why
　Ask me? What he wants you to know he will certainly tell you.
　It's not very generous to let a brother's success
　Fill you with spleen.

ROBERTO.　　　If you're imagining
　I'm envious of him you are wrong. I only want
　To know the exact nature of the bird
　Who has come back to crow here.

[47]

ANA-CLARA.   Human nature,
   And your brother's. Didn't you ever love him?

ROBERTO.   Of course.
   And want to still. That's the tormenting part of it.
   But the health of the present time is too critical
   To swallow tainted meat for the sake of the garnish.
                            [EDMONDO *looks out of a window.*

EDMONDO. Where's the Queen of all this? Are you coming,
   Ana-Clara? The kingdom's in suspense.

ANA-CLARA. In a moment.
                            [*She turns back to* ROBERTO.
                      How can I tell, after two not entirely
   Poised encounters, where the line divides
   Your shalt from your shalt-not? whether I should find it
   Just, or merely got out of the handbook?
   I can only say that Edmondo wants to please.
   You could start from there. You could suspend judgement
   On him, and perhaps on me till you know me better.—
   As I do on you, in spite of all provocation.
   You're an open question to me; we shall have
   To see how you answer, won't we?
              [*She smiles and goes into the Palazzo.* ROBERTO *stares after
              her.* GIOSETTA *has already entered.*

GIOSETTA.   A pretty tangle.
   Who's going to sort the grins from the groans?

ROBERTO.   Tell me,
   What do you think of the woman?

GIOSETTA.   Grazia
   Has been crying her eyes out.

ROBERTO.   What's wrong?

[48]

GIOSETTA.   If you can't think,
  Don't ask me to parade the reasons for you.

ROBERTO. I'd better go to her.

GIOSETTA.   She is all right now.
  She went to change her dress.
          [*Enter* GRAZIA. *She is wearing her best dress, some beads,*
          and has put her hair up, a flower in it.

ROBERTO.   I can see she has changed.
  What's all this for, Grazia?

GRAZIA [*gaily*].   All this for?
  In praise of life, of course. For the traveller's
  Return, and pots of gold, and the sound of the world
  Flying into the sun, whatever we ought to celebrate.
                                        [*She hugs* ROBERTO.
  Can't you stay and see what he's brought for you?

ROBERTO. I know what he's brought for me: enough to wonder
  What to do with.
          [GRAZIA *takes the flower from her hair and puts it in*
          ROBERTO's *buttonhole.*

GRAZIA.   Perhaps this was too much.
  But I've been to trouble's funeral. Poor thing,
  She's dead. For a while, anyway.
            [EDMONDO *looks out of a window, a glass in his hand.*

EDMONDO. Where's that wonder-to-behold Grazia?

GRAZIA. Here I am!
            [*She goes into the Palazzo.* ROBERTO *leans against the wall*
            near to GIOSETTA.

ROBERTO.   I can't altogether size her up.

GIOSETTA. You've known her ever since she existed. It's time
  You did.

[49]

ROBERTO. I don't mean Grazia. I was thinking
About Edmondo's wife. She has every
Characteristic you might expect in someone
Brought up never to doubt she was well chosen.
Drank homage with her mother's milk. Understands
Nothing with the air of an authority.
Plays the human game very skilfully
In expensive gloves. All that. But then there's something
I don't fathom. A pulse she is keeping hidden
Or doesn't know she possesses. Interesting.
Perhaps she has ambitions outside her class
Or why the hell did she marry my brother?
What made her go and do that? . . . She has made up her mind
Naturally enough not to approve of me.
Pompous and censorious, shaggy tempered
With a permanent grouch, that's what her verdict is.
I'm not going to change her short-sighted mind.
O God, Giosetta, why won't they see? I care
What they think and do, my bloody family.
Haven't we all learnt enough, without
Going back to learn it again? . . . What do you think of her?

GIOSETTA. I've done all the thinking I mean to do today.
Why don't you go and visit your sick?

[ROBERTO *looks at his watch, grunts, picks up his bag and
leaves* GIOSETTA *to her work.*

THE CURTAIN FALLS

END OF ACT ONE

[50]

ACT TWO

The courtyard, a day later. Evening. ANGELINO *is reading a news-*
paper outside the Osteria. GIOSETTA *comes out of her doorway.*

GIOSETTA. When do you think they will want to eat, Angelino?

ANGELINO. The minute they get back. They think we can hear
The rattle of stomachs right down the street.
What on earth is keeping them? I know
They'll have chewed the best off the bone of the news
Before we come near it.

GIOSETTA [*sitting*].   I'll take things slowly, then.
After the feast that 'Mondo gave us last night
I wouldn't want him to think we fed on clinkers.

                    [ANGELINO *has wandered out into the street.*

ANGELINO. There's no sign of them yet. It's really too bad.

GIOSETTA. It means we're getting old, if we start fussing
About the clock. When the war broke out
I had hardly begun to notice I wasn't young.
I was upstairs then looking out of the window.
Now I'm downstairs looking along a passage.
The war took the bottom two steps away.
It brings you down with a jolt.

ANGELINO.   Nonsense! Impatience
Isn't a sign of age, quite the opposite.
I want to get on with life, that's all; I'm restless
To know everything.

GIOSETTA.   You know what stopped you
From going to watch the practice-run yourself?

[51]

You weren't young enough to last the day
Without a three-hour siesta.

ANGELINO.   Ridiculous!
Age hasn't got anything to do with it.
I slept in the afternoon the day I was born.

GIOSETTA. You could find out what happened if you wanted to.
You like feeling neglected.

ANGELINO.   I don't at all.
I like to think I mean something. And if
They half loved me, they would have remembered
I was waiting here on tenterhooks for them.

GIOSETTA. While the war was on there weren't any young
Except the children, and only the very old
Were old. We were all equal, as far as thinking
What to expect out of life. But now we have been
Divided and sorted back into generations.

ANGELINO. I could still fall in love. Every so often
It crosses my mind. And now we're back to normal
I may give it some thought.

GIOSETTA.   Back to normal?
My dear man, ever since Edmondo came home
You haven't known where the ground was. Back to normal!
You can't decide where to put your poor feet.

ANGELINO. That's just it. The heart has been roused up.
The dreams I used to have are coming true.
You hear the ground under you purring again,
Warm, like a cat's back.—Suppose, Giosetta—
Not to be considered for many a day—
What would you do if your hopes gave out for Cesare?
Nothing to do with the present time, of course not.
But as time went by (if it did), as time went by,

[52]

Would you live alone, for the rest of your life?
I am really putting the question to the air.
I don't imagine you will hear it, not at all.

GIOSETTA. I got a message today. Somebody threw it
Out of a train that was passing through the station.
Tied to a piece of wood.

> [*She takes a piece of paper out of her pocket.*

ANGELINO.　　　　　From Cesare?
Where are my glasses? A good thing, a bad thing?

GIOSETTA. It's about Cesare. Whoever wrote it
Says: 'Dear Signora, I saw him at Bratislava
On June second.'

ANGELINO.　　　　Well, thank God, thank God.
And you kept it in your pocket! Cesare
Alive and well. It says he is well, does it?

GIOSETTA. No, there's no more. They can't even spell.
'Bratslavio' they've put. And they sucked their pencil.

ANGELINO. What a settling-up God's having this week!
Both of us within two days. Well, once
The bit's between His teeth things start to move!
And Grazia, isn't she in the seventh heaven?

GIOSETTA. I haven't told her. I don't want to tell her
Unless we're sure.

ANGELINO.　　　　But, woman, aren't we sure?

GIOSETTA. Maybe. She was singing this morning almost
Before she opened her eyes. Suppose I told her
And he didn't come to us.

ANGELINO.　　　　　　But, look, he's alive
And on his way home. Where else would he go?

GIOSETTA. Don't say anything, that's all. Forget I told you.

ANGELINO. I don't know how you contain yourself. However . . .
  [*He wanders towards the archway; then his feet give a sudden
  little skip.*
  On his way back! Bless the man. He's doing
  Better than my lot. Why hasn't Grazia hurried them?

GIOSETTA. She isn't with them.

ANGELINO.   Where is she, then?

GIOSETTA. In the Palazzo, being photographed.

ANGELINO. Photographed?

GIOSETTA.   Yes, Edmondo arranged it.
  He thinks she could have a career modelling fashions.
  Such dressing-up and grooming! It's best I keep
  Out of the way. She's like an eight-year-old
  Going off in white to her first communion.

ANGELINO. What a game!

GIOSETTA.   The last few years she hasn't
  Had much playing. She deserves a little fun.

ANGELINO. No complaints, have we?

GIOSETTA.   No, not many.
  She won't disappoint Cesare.

ANGELINO.   Neither her
  Nor either of you.

GIOSETTA.   We can't tell, can we?

ANGELINO. Certainly we can. My dear girl,
  You know yourself better than that.

GIOSETTA.   How do I?
  I only know what he saw in me—three years ago.
  Since then he has known things we haven't known.
  I may not answer any more.

[54]

ANGELINO.   What a way to talk!
  How can you say such a thing?

GIOSETTA.   I don't know why
  I did. I suppose it was because you seemed
  To be thinking of me as a woman.

ANGELINO.   I can't help it
  If that's what you put me in mind of. I guarantee
  Whatever he's been through he won't have lost
  The memory of you turning down the bedclothes.
  He will have kept you with him: like any other
  Marooned man who has to improvise
  His woman out of a desert, out of a breathing
  Cinder from the stove, or holding his boot
  In his hands as he used to hold your face, anything,
  I don't know what, anything to keep
  Body and soul together until he's rescued.

GIOSETTA. Trust you to make an opera out of it.
  I'm bothered enough, without having to be
  Madam Butterfly with the boot face.
  What are we going to recognize in each other,
  That's all I wonder.

ANGELINO.   Well, you needn't wonder.
  You'll mend the world for him, if he wants it mending,
  Or nobody can. Goodness me, if *you*
  Start wondering what you are, what happens to the rest of us?
        [GIOSETTA *has thought of going indoors but is impelled to
        talk.*

GIOSETTA. If we could have married, it might have felt
  Something solid, divided and come together.
  In the early years whenever I went to confession
  And had to call our love a sin
  I felt I was being unfaithful to him with God.

[55]

Cesare laughed, and said it was God who was jealous,
Not him. But when they took him away
I even thought it might be the punishment
For our life together. It wasn't a good thought,
To my mind, anyway. Only, if we were married . . .

ANGELINO. Yes, well, but that wasn't the way it was.

GIOSETTA. His wife has always been an ill woman, almost
From the day they were married. And now, Alfio says,
The arthritis has tightened its knots terribly.
But when Cesare was there it seemed to be
Hardly more than a fear of being made love to.
He got it in his head he was crucifying her,
And hated the life in his own body.
It was like having a foul tattoo-mark on him
Which he couldn't get rid of. He began to avoid
Good innocent people (what he imagined were)
As though his presence was insulting them:
Children in the street, even his son. His mind
Lost its way altogether. He even felt
The sky draw away from him. He said that once.

ANGELINO. Poor Cesare!

GIOSETTA.   So he ran for his life.
He has been happy here—not always happy.
Questions would come rolling over him
Like tanks every now and then: was he sure
She was better off without him? Was a mad
Father better than none for Alfio?
Had he run from what God wanted of him?
It was then he would go drinking.

    Enter PIERO MARTINI, *a photographer, from the Palazzo.*

PIERO.   Ah, signora!
She has been an enchantment, your little girl.

You have a major artist for a daughter.
Really! She has the secret: plasticity,
An intuitive body—and *bones*. Honestly,
I've never known such movement in stillness.

GIOSETTA.   Fidgety?

PIERO. Certainly not, you should be very proud of her.

GIOSETTA. If she has bones I suppose so.

ANGELINO.   I'm surprised
    She didn't mention it to us.

PIERO.   Use your eyes—
    Here she is—you'll see what I'm talking about.

> [GRAZIA *comes into the doorway, elegant; the* LADY'S
> MAID *beside her, making last adjustments.* GRAZIA *pulls a
> face at* GIOSETTA.

PIERO. Stay just where you are, Grazia. There. Imagine
    You have come out to feel the evening air—
    Relax in it, breathe it in—

GRAZIA [*breathing in*].   Mother,
    Is there something on the stove?

GIOSETTA.   That's all right,
    Nothing to spoil.

PIERO.   Never mind about the stove.
    Turn a little to your—good; I don't have to tell you.
    Chin a mill-imetre—marvellous. That's perfect.
    We'll make each other's fortunes. Now, I wonder,
    What would be—ah, yes! Let's see you over there,
    Over there in front of the broken plaster.

> [GRAZIA *dances a step or two, kisses* GIOSETTA, *and goes
> obediently to where* PIERO *points.*

PIERO. I want to make just a bare statement of texture,
    A comment on flesh, silk and stone.

C   [57]

Look dead straight into the camera. Economize
On Body as much as you can. Try to think
Vertically, narrow. . . . If you're going to laugh,
Grazia, we're destroyed. I want to see you
Without history or class: a pure, simple
Human idea without human fallibility.

ROBERTO *and* ANA-CLARA *come into the archway.*

ANGELINO. He doesn't ask much! He certainly puts her through it.

PIERO. Superb. Just one more. We're almost there.

ROBERTO. Will someone explain?

GRAZIA.   Oh, Bobo, I'm being shown
How to be economical. Isn't that good?

ROBERTO. In that high-class rig-out? What's going on?

ANA-CLARA. An idea that Edmondo had, an experiment
To see if she's photogenic. It occurred to him
She could model fashions.

ROBERTO.   Oh, *did* it?

ANA-CLARA.   And why not?

PIERO. I pick words gingerly like a rose out of thorns,
But this girl has genius. She is going to start
A revolution in the appearance of women.
Mark what I say, by nineteen forty-seven
No one will recognize his own sister.

ANGELINO. That seems a pity.

ROBERTO.   Thanks, now pack up and go.

PIERO. My instructions don't come from you, as I understand it.

GRAZIA. We can lose the last one. And the light is going.
Anyway I'm tired of being other people.

PIERO. Other people! You couldn't be other people.
Other people are going to be you.

[58]

And every film-producer worth his salt
Will want to be the first to let the world see it.

ROBERTO. For God's sake go, will you? Take yourself off.

ANGELINO. That's no way to talk, when the young man
Has gone to such trouble. There you are, gun-happy
Again!

GRAZIA [*to* PIERO]. We're easily startled. But thank you
For all your patience. I'm sorry I laughed so much.

PIERO. Be strong, my dear. No one can alter destiny.
Good-evening.
            [*They all wish him a good-evening as he bows and goes.*

ANA-CLARA [*to* ROBERTO]. You bully.

GRAZIA.   He went quite pale.

ANA-CLARA.   And then he faded
On the blowing of the horn.

ANGELINO.   What a way to behave!

ROBERTO. Yes, I'm sorry. I should really have let him
Wind himself off with the spool. I'm sorry, Grazia.
I suddenly took against him.

GRAZIA.   You came back
Too late to catch the beauty of the joke.

GIOSETTA. I shall leave you two to fight it out between you.

GRAZIA. I'm going to change into myself again.
            [GRAZIA *goes into the Palazzo,* GIOSETTA *into her apart-
            ment.*

ANGELINO. You didn't have to bark at the wretched fellow.
Anyhow, what happened at the practice-run?

ROBERTO. I haven't heard. Aren't they home yet?

[59]

ANGELINO.   No.
   I can't understand it. What have you been doing?
   Going round with your brimstone and treacle?

ROBERTO. Yes.

ANA-CLARA.   And with a new Sister of Mercy.
   I'm trying to keep tomorrow unspied on.

ANGELINO. That's it—let the great day take you unawares.
                    [ANGELINO *goes into the Osteria.*

ANA-CLARA. The great day when I weigh the actual event
   Against my dream of it. I have great hopes.
   And tell me, bear, why shouldn't Grazia blossom?

ROBERTO. Doesn't she please you?

ANA-CLARA.   Of course she pleases me.

ROBERTO. Then why want to change her? What do you all
   Think you're doing? I could kill Edmondo!
   Make her a model! Turn her into a clothes horse!

ANA-CLARA. Better that than a pack-horse.

ROBERTO.   Which isn't
   The alternative. Just tell me what went on in you
   All this afternoon?

ANA-CLARA.   Went on?

ROBERTO.   It shocked you,
   Didn't it, to see the conditions they live in?

ANA-CLARA. No, I wasn't shocked. I tried to feel
   Responsible because I knew you expected it.
   But no, most of the time—most of the time—
   Well, I was happy.

ROBERTO.   Happy!

ANA-CLARA.   Yes; so were they.
   You made them laugh. You somehow changed each room

[60]

Into a little ark bobbing on the flood.
That certainly opened my eyes. I wasn't to know
You kept a sense of humour curled up
In your black bag.

ROBERTO.   I see. So it was all
A big entertainment. I might have expected it.
But when I saw how at ease with them you were
At once, and they with you, I let myself
Think I'd achieved something.

ANA-CLARA.   So you had.
And what you most wanted to achieve.
You didn't really think I should come home
And sell all my jewellery, or so fall out
Of love with life I should never eat caviare.
You wanted me to see you at work, your cuffs
Turned back, relaxed in your own element,
And obviously worshipped. And I saw this, marvellously.

ROBERTO. You're so female, it's almost obscene.
How did the male genes come to miss you?
Reduce everything to personalities
If that's all you're capable of. I'm disappointed.

ANA-CLARA. I never met anybody so ready to take
Admiration for mockery. I don't know why you object
To being generous to me, and human—the very
Charm in you that does them good.
If you lectured *them* as you lectured me on the way
They would all think death a happy release. You came
Far nearer to prodding my social conscience awake
By letting me see they loved you, than with all
That rhapsody of statistics. What touched me was
That you wanted me to see the work you were doing,
Wanted *me* to see it. And not as one

[61]

Of the unconverted being offered salvation;
As a woman welcome to share it. You don't need
To look so crestfallen.

ROBERTO.   I need to look
Exactly what I feel, mortified.
What in hell did I think I was doing
Exhibiting their lives to you, like specimens?
It serves me right that what impressed you most
Was my performance as a clown.

ANA-CLARA.   I didn't say so.

ROBERTO. You have my full leave to. The whole thing
Was a prat-falling comedy. There I was
Solemnly delivering a shock
For your own good, and I'm the one who gets it.
I'm the one whose dignity's flat on its chin.

> *Enter* ANGELINO *with a large tablecloth.*

ANGELINO. They can't be much longer now unless they're dead.
We may as well lay.

> [ROBERTO *and* ANA-CLARA, *at the table, hardly notice
> him.*

ANA-CLARA.   You don't know where your strength is.
You deploy in the wrong direction.

ROBERTO.   But nevertheless
This doesn't let *you* out. If I was the clown
You were the undiscriminating audience.

ANGELINO. Elbows, please.

> [ROBERTO *absent-mindedly raises his elbows so that*
> ANGELINO *can spread the cloth.* ANA-CLARA, *also with
> her mind elsewhere, gets up and helps.*

ROBERTO.   I'm thoroughly baffled by you.
You were so right with them, and you come away

[62]

Apparently quite untroubled. There seem to be
Two totally different people in you.

ANA-CLARA. Only two? Isn't that rather sub-normal?
You don't have to condemn yourself for anything.
You may have set out to use them as facts against me
But, if so, flesh and blood got the better of you,
Affection triumphed.

ANGELINO.   Do I hear them coming?

ROBERTO. Who?

ANGELINO.   Edmondo and Luigi.

ANA-CLARA.   Yes, here they are.
I suppose I should go and change.

              EDMONDO *and* LUIGI *come into the archway.*

ANGELINO. So you've managed to get here at last. About time, too.

LUIGI. Prepare yourselves for a shock. Cambriccio
Is out of the race.

ANA-CLARA.   Oh, no!

ANGELINO.   You can't mean that!

EDMONDO. Yes, out of it. We've been down at the hospital.

ROBERTO. What happened? What's the report on him?

EDMONDO.   He had
Some sort of vertigo—came off the horse,
Anyway; and got kicked on the head.
When we left him he was still unconscious.
                    [GRAZIA *has come out of the Palazzo.*

ANGELINO. What a disaster! The end of a career,
Gone on too long. What a terrible thing the years are.
There's the finish of all our bright hopes.

EDMONDO. Don't panic. I'll find a substitute.
I've got some contacts who can take care of this.

[63]

ROBERTO. Of course he has.

EDMONDO.   I'll put a call through now.

ANGELINO. What a blessing to have you, when the devil turns
    ugly.
    I can't believe it. Who won, then?

LUIGI.   Alfio did.
    He's three times more impressive up on a horse
    Than he is on the ground. Without Cambriccio
    We haven't a chance if he rides like this afternoon.
    Except, thank goodness, 'Mondo seems indestructible.
    Excuse me—I want to study his methods.
                    [LUIGI *follows* EDMONDO *into the Palazzo.*

ANGELINO. Shall we be in his way if I come, too?
    I can't wait about. Grazia, we must tell your mother.

GRAZIA. Isn't it awful? I'll tell her.
                [*Exit* GRAZIA. ANGELINO *goes to the Palazzo door.*

ANGELINO.   What a minefield
    Life is! One minute you're taking a stroll in the sun,
    The next your legs and arms are all over the hedge.
    There's no dignity in it.
                                [*Exit* ANGELINO.

ANA-CLARA.   How wretched for Edmondo
    After all his contriving.

ROBERTO.   Wretched for Edmondo!
    He arranged the whole thing for his own prestige,
    But the parish has to suffer for it. Of course
    You're not concerned with them, the real victims:
    Only the blow to poor Edmondo's vanity.

ANA-CLARA. Will you stop bullying me?

ROBERTO.   No, I won't.

[64]

I should like to haul you by that elegant neck
Up and down the land, till you saw the truth.

ANA-CLARA. You want the truth. All right, then you shall have it.
I've taken enough preaching.—I was born
In a Lisbon slum, in a room more polluted,
More of a crowded dungeon under a moat,
Than anywhere you have shown me today. At five
I was a better beggar than all the nuns
Of Portugal, and as sharp as an adult rat.

ROBERTO. If you want to take the wind out of my sails
Invent something believable.

ANA-CLARA.   Do you think
I like giving up the part? I was loving it.
It was only your bloody nagging made me tell you.

ROBERTO. How could you love it if you knew it was false?

ANA-CLARA. Oh, false! What's false, what's real? That squalid
childhood
Lied about every living thing that was in me.

ROBERTO. If it ever existed. If it ever could have existed.

ANA-CLARA. You don't believe in people who find their own way.
You suspect them.

ROBERTO.   Not necessarily.

ANA-CLARA. Oh, yes you do. You don't trust what they are now
Unless you know how they came to be what they are.

ROBERTO. I don't ask how you came to be. I'm content to marvel.

ANA-CLARA. You mean, to wonder; curious to know
What code I offended on the upward climb.
Well, you shall hear.

ROBERTO.   I don't want to hear.
I accept your self-creation.

[65]

ANA-CLARA.   I'm not chancing
Those under-the-brow looks you give Edmondo.

ROBERTO. You wouldn't get them.

ANA-CLARA.   I know you couldn't choose.
Can imagination's environment
Alter heredity? You can't help asking.
—On my fifteenth birthday I went to live
With a young actor. He was like a redeemer
Piercing the darkness for me. If it wasn't
Morality, it was always love and always
Learning.

ROBERTO.   If you love you learn, a simple truth.

ANA-CLARA. He thought he could make me an actress, and for two
Patient years he taught me to speak and move.
But fury and tears took over. The characters
We played together began to seem ridiculous,
Making their gestures in the nine-foot square
Of a rented room, lit by a fifty-watt bulb.
I began to crave for reality.

ROBERTO.   Whatever that is,
As you said just now. You mean you wanted
To have a genuine victory over life.

ANA-CLARA. Something was dancing on ahead of me.
I fell in love with knowledge, which appeared to me
In the body of a university lecturer.
I was a kind of pupil-mistress. Dived
Into the poets, or tangled with philosophers,
Or lay back and let the mind of music
Do my comprehending of life's hard things.
I felt limitless and very happy.

ROBERTO.   But not
For ever.

ANA-CLARA. No, not for ever. He exchanged
Our bed for a Chair in Comparative Anatomy
In Salamanca.

ROBERTO.   A careerist, if ever there was one.

ANA-CLARA. I felt lost for a while; taught Portuguese
To foreign businessmen. Which brought me
To Edmondo.

ROBERTO.   Ah, Edmondo!

ANA-CLARA.   Ah, Edmondo.
This time I could love from a level start.
He and I were climbing the same pitch,
Though Edmondo had the impressive male advantage
Of being ruthless. Bless him, he could have bought
A real duchess, but he settled for silver-gilt.
And now no matter how far I stretched my arms
No walls were there, nothing to frown on me.

ROBERTO. Then what do you shy away from?

ANA-CLARA.   What do you mean?

ROBERTO. I never saw a woman whose eyes were so transparent.
Every half-thought flies past there naked.
At first I thought you were over-bred, but now
You've proved me wrong. What is it that puts your ears back?
                    [ANA-CLARA *is silent for a moment.*

ANA-CLARA. Can anyone be at perfect ease with life?

ROBERTO. With life, or with himself—which do you mean?
I suppose life is willing, when we can find
What it's groping for. This afternoon I felt
Somehow that we seemed to belong to each other,
And to all the rest of them as well.

[67]

ANA-CLARA.   You see?
You are understanding at last why I was happy.
We belonged to each other.

ROBERTO.   While the illusion lasted.

ANA-CLARA. You don't give truth a chance to declare itself.
Poor foetus in the womb, condemned as illusion!
It had the kick of life for *me*, I may say.
Your hands were capable and kind. They made
The worst things . . . in a way serviceable.
Without touching me, you took me in your arms
And lifted my body across a new threshold.
Exactly as you meant to.

ROBERTO.   How do you know that?
Did you see any professional negligence?

ANA-CLARA. No; your concentration was part of the love-making.
An oblique seduction can be very successful.
This one was.

ROBERTO.   I could feel you charging my body
From any distance. What are we to do?

ANA-CLARA. Are you asking that seriously?

ROBERTO. Don't breathe on me, or I shall break.
                    [*If they were not in a public place they would kiss.*
          Enter from the Palazzo, EDMONDO, LUIGI, ANGELINO.
                    EDMONDO *looks at* ANA-CLARA *and* ROBERTO.

LUIGI. Don't fret, Edmondo. We all know you can do it.

EDMONDO. I'm not fretting.

LUIGI.   We shall leave you alone
When this long-distance call has come through;
We may be curdling the magic.

ANA-CLARA.   Aren't you having
Any luck?

EDMONDO. It's taking time, that's all.

ANGELINO. Who can wonder? Even the Creator
Took a week over us—too quick,
A scamped job in some ways. We can't expect
A Cambriccio on every telegraph-pole.

EDMONDO [*to* ANA-CLARA]. How was your afternoon? Profitable?

ANA-CLARA. Friendly. I wish yours had been happier.
But I never yet knew you to fail in a crisis.

> [ANA-CLARA *goes into the Palazzo.*

ROBERTO. Ah, well, we shall have to fall back on Luigi.

LUIGI. Fall back on me? In what way, fall back on me?

ROBERTO. Aren't you the nearest thing to a cavalryman
'n this parish of foot-sloggers?

ANGELINO.   Have *Luigi* ride?

ROBERTO. Yes, why not?

EDMONDO.   You don't need to get frantic.
It's being dealt with.

ROBERTO.   Well, if the black mass fails
You might give a thought to our off-white hope here.
We need someone prepared to spill his guts
To stop us losing, not a coerced celebrity,
Blackguarded into coming, with his heart not in it.
Here's your chance, Luigi, to pull in the votes
At the next election. The man of gold
Who slew the dragon for us. It's high time
One of us gave Edmondo a run for his money.

> [ROBERTO *goes into the Osteria.*

LUIGI. Here, wait a minute! It's all very well.

ANGELINO. Do you think you could do it? What a stroke it
would be!

[69]

Why don't you tell Edmondo about the time
Your jeep sank in the mud, or the sand-dune,
Whatever it was. He commandeered a horse
And was up with the head of the mechanized unit
Before they had travelled half a kilometre.
Or was it a camel?

LUIGI.   A camel. All the same,
It would certainly be a great political platform—
As long as I won. But there's the horse: you can't
Be sure how the horse's vote is going to go.
And, worse than that, there's Alfio Scapare.
It would take a thunderbolt to beat him.

> [ETTORE, *the chauffeur, comes in from the street. He
> carries a bundle of clothes and a pair of shoes.*

ETTORE. Excuse me, if you're talking about Scapare:
Here's all of him that's free to get about
Just now.

EDMONDO. What's this?

ETTORE.   His shirt, trousers, and shoes, sir.
The boys said they weren't taking any chances.
They want you to look after them.

EDMONDO.   You mean
They've picked him up?

ETTORE.   He strolled up here, sat down
In the local café, and started asking everybody
About his father.

LUIGI.   Magnificent! He's gone mad.

ANGELINO. After all we told him about what would happen
If they found him here!

[70]

EDMONDO. Fetch him, Ettore.
I'll have a word with him. We'll try to avoid
The Dragons breathing fire all over us.

ETTORE. You don't mean to let him ride, do you, sir?

EDMONDO. I won't let him win, at any rate.

LUIGI. He knows we're amiable; you can persuade him.

ETTORE. Very well, sir.

LUIGI. You will need these, won't you?
[ETTORE *takes the clothes, and exit.*

ANGELINO. What a stroke of luck he should be born so simple
And trusting! Our hopes are looking up again.

LUIGI. What will you do, 'Mondo? Make him listen to money?

EDMONDO. Leave it to me.

ANGELINO. We certainly don't want
To have any violence, fighting in the streets
Or anything like that. Diplomacy is the way.

Enter GRAZIA.

GRAZIA. Mother wants to know if you're ready to eat now?

LUIGI. We're ready for anything!

GRAZIA. Have you found somebody?

ANGELINO. We think there's a light on the way.

LUIGI. Enough to feed by,
At least. We can sit down and be nourished.
[GRAZIA *goes in.* ANGELINO *pours wine.*

ANGELINO. Now that we've guessed who isn't going to win
We come back to the question of who will.
How do you feel about trusting your brother to it?
You never know, he might have something of *you*
In him, if he was given the chance.

[71]

EDMONDO.   You don't
   Trust me to get us out of this, is that it?
   If we have to scrape the barrel, well, here he is.
LUIGI. It's nice to know I'm valued, that's encouraging.
   I know what you mean, though. I haven't ever
   Brought anything off yet, not, at any rate,
   On a scale you'd recognize. But the smell of success
   Has always been in my nose, hasn't it, daddo?
   One happy lurch and I should be into it.
                         [He pats himself on the belly.
   And I'm not in bad condition, really; not more
   Than two months pregnant. I'll win the race or die.
   Put your shirt on it, or my shroud on me.

            [GIOSETTA enters with food on a tray, followed by GRAZIA
            with another tray. They put the food on the table. ROBERTO
            comes out from the Osteria.

GIOSETTA. Grazia says you are all more cheerful.
   What's the situation now?
ANGELINO.   Shall we tell them?
EDMONDO. Why not? They're going to know as soon as he gets
   here.
ANGELINO. Young Alfio crossed our frontier this evening;
   They've got him under lock and key.
ROBERTO.   They have?
GIOSETTA. Then I think it's shameful, I think it's wicked!
   It isn't fair to treat him like that, you bandits!
ANGELINO. Now, wait and hear. He walked right into Rosario's
   And started asking questions about Cesare.
GRAZIA. Then I'm glad they caught him!
GIOSETTA.   You're as bad as they are.
   It's a mean, brutal trick. I'd rather lose
   All my money than have this happen to him.

[72]

GRAZIA. I told him, I told him to leave it alone.

EDMONDO. Don't get so worked up, Giosetta. Nobody
Is going to stop him riding in the race.

GIOSETTA. You're going to bribe him to lose, then.

EDMONDO.   I'm going
To talk to him. We'll come to an understanding.

ROBERTO. Where's Ana-Clara? Has anyone thought of calling her?
  [LUIGI, *who has been touching his toes, comes to the table.*

LUIGI. The only question is, will he accept?

GRAZIA. No, I don't think he will.

GIOSETTA.   It's possible.

ANGELINO. You think he might?

GIOSETTA.   I was thinking of something he said.
  [ROBERTO *meets* ANA-CLARA *at the Palazzo doorway.*

ROBERTO. I was on the way to find you.

ANA-CLARA.   By a silly mischance
I've made the future more insecure than ever.

EDMONDO. What's happened now?

ANA-CLARA.   I looked at the new moon
Through a closed window.

ROBERTO.   And why shouldn't you?

ANA-CLARA. It's bad luck. An English salesman told me.
Whenever he saw the new moon through glass
Business dropped. You must all look at it now
To change my luck; bow to heaven and wish.

EDMONDO. It's how the English keep up their exports.

LUIGI. Where is the little sliver, then?

ANA-CLARA.   Up there,
Balanced on the roof. You see? Invest your wishes.

ANGELINO. With all *we* want, it will be enough to sink it.

ANA-CLARA. 'Gentle Siena evening: a light-giving pearl
'In the proud cloak of Provenzan Salvani
'And the moon curved like a begging hand
'Beside the Commune tower. . . .'
Your poet Fiorentino.

[*A silence, everyone with his own thoughts.*

GRAZIA. I don't think mother wished.

GIOSETTA.   Oh, yes, I did.
I wished you would all get on and eat your food
Before it's cold as charity.

ROBERTO.   Good appetite.

EDMONDO. I bet I know what each one of you was wishing.
Do you want me to try?

ANA-CLARA.   No.

LUIGI.   All right, then, tell us.

EDMONDO. To start with, father was wishing life was all smiles
Like it was this morning.

ANA-CLARA.   Don't you tell him, angel,
Or it never will be.

EDMONDO.   Luigi wished he could win
The race, standing up on the horse's back
Shouting 'Citizens of Siena!'

LUIGI.   Well, of course.

EDMONDO. Roberto—he's the tricky customer.
He was probably wishing he could steal my wife.

ANGELINO. Now, 'Mondo! I won't have that, even as a joke.

EDMONDO. It was in bad taste, was it? Excuse me.
Excuse me, Roberto. Suppose we move on
Into the clearer waters of Grazia's mind.

[74]

She wished for fame and riches, to spin the world
Round her like a dirndl in a dance.

GRAZIA. No.

EDMONDO.   Oh, yes. With all this Cambriccio trouble
I haven't even asked you how you got on.
They say Piero Martini's a great artist.
I meant to have got back in time to talk to him.

GRAZIA. He was here for hours.

ANGELINO.   He said our pony had genius.

EDMONDO. Did he? I thought he'd like her. So will everyone.
Imagine the rustle in the Via Veneto.
'Did you see who that was? Grazia Scapare!'—
Who will care about the moon, that old graffito
Chalked up there? There's a new planet in the sky,
Discovered by the keen-eyed astronomer
Edmondo Bruno, all set to plot
Her trajectory across the skies. Excited?

ROBERTO. Just what I thought—a business proposition!

EDMONDO. What's wrong with that? Individuality
Is a very valuable property;
It needs professional handling.

ROBERTO.   Exploitation.

ANGELINO. Now for heaven's sake, don't you start shooting
Your quills again. We want to eat in peace,
Not have to peer twice at every mouthful
In case we're spitted. You haven't been looking pretty
Since the night of the storm.

ROBERTO.   Maybe not.

ANGELINO.   Just be
Your usual sunny bloody-minded self.

[75]

GRAZIA. Luigi, what's the matter? You're not eating anything.

LUIGI. I know, but I may have to ride the horse tomorrow.
You can't eat, with something like that on your mind.

GIOSETTA. I doubt if any of you would have noticed
If I'd grilled the horse *tonight*.

ANGELINO. But every mouthful
Gives a memory to my palate, Giosetta!
Come along, we must drink your health, we certainly must.
                    [*They drink* GIOSETTA's *health.*

ANA-CLARA. Grazia isn't the only one with talent.

ROBERTO. Why don't you sell Giosetta to the Grand Hotel,
Edmondo?

EDMONDO. For God's sake! Let's get this over with.
You resent me taking care of Grazia's career.
That's just too bad.

ROBERTO. If you'd only try and make
One small effort to comprehend something.
You thought you could come back to where you grew up
And take it over. You can't; it doesn't exist.
It's gone, like the old wine that father lost.
We're having to make do with something nondescript
Till a new vintage is given time to mature.
But, even so, nothing is the same.
We've all been dragged out of bed and shot, in some way,
By what we've seen, or what we were made to do
To stop another grotesque world being born.
We owe such a debt to the dead ones, it will take
Generations to pay back.

EDMONDO. Don't fool yourself,
Nothing's the same! It's only too pathetically
The same, exactly as I remember it.

And if we listen to you it always will be.
I came home to change all your lives for you,
And a lot of thanks I get, from you, anyway.

ROBERTO. If you owned all the silver in Potosi
You couldn't touch our trouble.

LUIGI.   Why couldn't he?
If we attract big business here, encourage
Free enterprise, build up heavy industry,
Pump money into the dry cisterns,
Prosperity snowballs.

ROBERTO.   Into whose pocket?
Up and down the land how many will profit?
You've never told us what your business was
In Portugal.

EDMONDO.   Raw materials. Wolfram, mainly.

ROBERTO. And you sold it where, to Germany?

EDMONDO. Not only Germany: America, England, Japan. . . .

ROBERTO. Anybody willing to buy! My God, don't you
Believe in anything in life except money?

EDMONDO. At least there's no blood on my hands, like some people.
It's not bad to have made a good life in a world gone crazy.
       [ROBERTO *leans across the table and grabs* EDMONDO *by
       the shirt.*

ROBERTO. I'll kill you!

ANGELINO.   Sit down, Roberto!
Why did you have to bring up the subject? A nice
Meal time you're giving us. If this
Goes on I shall go to bed. Why can't we
Have some music, eh? I'd even welcome
(Saint Cecilia forgive me) a song from Luigi.

[77]

ROBERTO. And you think you can bring your filthy money here
   And buy us over again into the old
   Discredited welter of greeds we've just been fighting
   Our way out of! And drag Grazia into it!
   Into a rehash of the old tribal dance
   Designed to show off their beads and feathers.
   Grazia, the best one of all of us,
   Who has lived these years without a mark against her.

       [GRAZIA, *suddenly agitated, starts collecting the plates.*

GRAZIA. It isn't true!

ROBERTO.   Yes, it is, it's quite true.
   And Edmondo thinks he's giving you a future
   To have you dressing and undressing for a doll-headed
   Decadent lot of fashion-hunters. It makes me
   Shudder. That's all I'm saying.

EDMONDO.   All *you*'re saying.
   How about Grazia? What does she say?

ROBERTO. I can trust Grazia.

ANA-CLARA.   Well, if you trust Grazia,
   What are you so concerned about?

              Enter ETTORE *with a dishevelled* ALFIO.

LUIGI.   Hold on,
   Here's our friend. Good evening.

ANGELINO.   Yes—well—
   We must leave him to Edmondo.

GIOSETTA.   It's a shame.

EDMONDO. I hear that you've made trouble for yourself,
   Scapare.

ALFIO.   Who's at the back of this—are you?
   If so I want compensation for assault!

[78]

I've been beaten up, stripped, and shut in a cellar.
There are laws against that. It's about time
This slum found out there isn't a war on now—

ROBERTO. Everything's a war.

ALFIO.   —we don't have to get
Permission to walk about your town! I'll sue you!

EDMONDO. Suppose you stop shouting, and we can think
How to deal with the mess you've got yourself into.

ALFIO. I don't wonder none of you was able to tell me
Who betrayed my father. The whole district
Is a crawling snake's nest!

GRAZIA [crossing with plates]. I told you to keep
Your fingers out of it.

GIOSETTA.   I expect he's hungry.

EDMONDO. He and I have something we have to discuss first.
         [EDMONDO leads ALFIO away. GIOSETTA follows GRAZIA
         with the second tray.

ANGELINO. I mustn't start feeling sorry for him, when fate
Has delivered him into our hands. I'll fetch more wine,
We're going to need it, if only to cry into.
         [ANGELINO takes the empty bottles to the Osteria.

LUIGI. I think I'll take a walk while this is going on.
It's a bit embarrassing, really. I'll warn the horse
We may have a closer relationship tomorrow.
         [Exit LUIGI. EDMONDO and ALFIO come downstage.

ALFIO. All I want to hear from you is an apology.

EDMONDO. Because you took it into your infant head
To cross into enemy territory? You're mad.
It's lucky for you you fell into good hands.
All you're going to lose by it is the race.

[79]

ALFIO. Are you trying to twist my arm?

EDMONDO.   To fill your pocket.
   Money in your wallet can carry you farther
   Than a cheering crowd can. I'm prepared, what's more,
   To give you a steadier currency than money:
   American cigarettes. As you're a Scapare
   I'll give you ten thousand Lucky Strike.
   That's wampum anywhere, and gold in Naples.
   The Black Market price, if you don't happen
   To be familiar with it, is, as at this moment—

ALFIO. You can't bribe me. I'm not going to break
   Faith with the men who hired me.

EDMONDO.   You did that, son,
   The moment you sat down in Rosario's.
   If we can't do business, I simply have to return you
   To your captors, and I can't vouch for them.
   This will be a profitable experience,
   Teaching you more than you learnt in all your years.
   Not only your pocket, your character will benefit.

ALFIO. Character! Give up trusting anybody,
   Is that what you mean? And never be worthy again
   Of being trusted! No, you can't make me do it.

EDMONDO. I suggest you calm down with some mental activity
   Like a simple sum: if a cigarette and a half
   Cost a lira and a half. . . . You can take your time.
   We have all the night ahead of us.

ALFIO.   You swine!
        [EDMONDO *wanders towards the table as* ANGELINO *comes
        back with wine.*

EDMONDO. That's well managed, exactly at half-time.
   How about you two, staring into empty glasses
   Like unemployed crystal-gazers? Open a bottle.

[80]

ANA-CLARA. What success are you having with our destiny?

ANGELINO. How is he taking it?

EDMONDO.   He's thinking it over.
  The temperature is cooling.—A drink, Scapare?

> [ALFIO, *leaning against the far wall, shakes his head.*
> EDMONDO *fills his own glass and returns.*

ROBERTO. I'm sweating in sympathy with him, the poor devil.

ANGELINO. The hard birth that mamma had with you,
  That was terrible.

ANA-CLARA.   Was he resisting the world
  Even then?

ROBERTO.   I was giving it a hard look.

EDMONDO [*to* ALFIO]. Well, Scapare, have you done your arith-
  metic?

> [ALFIO *gives a Neapolitan gesture of succumbing to fate:
> the base of the palm of the hand strikes a glancing blow on
> the forehead, ricocheting off to describe an arc in the air, the
> gesture finishing above the head and to the side, palm upward
> to the sky; the shoulders are shrugged, the head on one side
> towards the flung arm; the other arm bent upwards, the hand
> palm upward, the fingers spread; the mouth drawn down,
> the lips pursed.*

EDMONDO. What does that mean in Naples?

ALFIO. What in hell can I do about it?
  There are things you don't know, things that give you
  An unfair advantage over me. Otherwise,
  I can tell you, you'd never be able to buy me.
  But I'm cornered. The pain my mother is in all the time
  Plays right into your hands. I need the money.

EDMONDO. There you are, you see, I'm acting providence.
  I'm rather good at it.

[81]

ALFIO.   The doctor has said
    Only one thing can help her, a new drug
    Called cortisone. It's just possible to get it
    From America, at a price. The cost of it
    Would pay for half a minute of a war,
    A minor royalty's ransom. No other reason
    In the world would make me surrender.

EDMONDO.   Ah, there's nothing
    Like the influence of a good mother.
    I'm glad to have been of some help.

ALFIO.   You've destroyed me.

EDMONDO. Nothing of the sort. Come over and have a drink.
    You can afford to relax now, and enjoy yourself.

            Enter GIOSETTA *and* GRAZIA *with trays.*

ALFIO. I don't feel like company. I don't know
    Who I am any more. I'm not fit
    To be with other people, anyway.

EDMONDO. Nonsense. You've never done so much good
    By one decision in your life before.
    Come on.

GIOSETTA. What has become of Luigi?

ROBERTO. He's gone off to use his charm on the horse.
                         [EDMONDO *brings* ALFIO *to the table.*

EDMONDO. Here's a good friend who could do with a drink.

ANGELINO. And he shall have it, bless him. Alfio,
    Hard decisions make ready minds. There you are.

EDMONDO. Let's drink his health. Happy days, Scapare,
    And no looking back. Always onward and upward.

ANGELINO. That's it. Fame and fortune.

GIOSETTA [*kissing* ALFIO'*s forehead*].   Poor Alfio.

ROBERTO. To the conscience-haunted night that we deserve.

EDMONDO. Now if only that call would come through—

GRAZIA.   Alfio,
I'm sorry for you, and it's my fault.

ALFIO.   What do you mean?

GRAZIA. I could have stopped you getting into this trouble.

ALFIO. No, you couldn't. I had to try and find out.

GRAZIA. Not if I had told you what you wanted to know.

GIOSETTA. Grazia!

ALFIO.   For God's sake! Why didn't you, then?

GRAZIA. Oh, I wish I could go away from here! I'm sick
Of the smell of the war in our hair, on everything I touch.
I want to be where nothing reminds me of anything.
Rome! I could lose myself there, couldn't I
Edmondo? I should feel better there.
Not to be quite real, however absurd—
A fancy person, someone else's invention,
Whose clothes, even, aren't her own clothes.
I'll go, if they invite me.

EDMONDO.   Of course you will!

ALFIO. But you know who gave him away! Tell me Grazia:
I promise I won't make trouble. I think I deserve
To know, after what's happened. Who betrayed him?

GRAZIA. I did.

GIOSETTA.   No, Grazia.

GRAZIA.   Yes. I did.

ANGELINO. I never heard such nonsense!

GRAZIA   I told Rosa,
Rosa Levanti. Of all people! I told her

[83]

We had him here. I knew Rosa could never
Keep quiet about anything, and yet
I babbled it all out to her.

ANGELINO.   My dear, my dear,
There was no harm, with a family friend like Rosa.

GRAZIA. I went back and begged her to forget
I had ever told her. She laughed and promised.
But if God had struck her dumb there and then
I had done it, I betrayed him. Now you all know.

GIOSETTA. Why didn't you tell me, you silly girl? How could you
Make yourself so miserable? Is that all
You think of me—someone you can't confide in?

GRAZIA. Sometimes, later on, I would almost forget
Now and then, for a little while. Because no one knew.
If I had told you, whenever we were together
I should all the time have known it was in your mind.

GIOSETTA. Oh, no! Grazia, no one would have blamed you.

GRAZIA. Say I was still a child! That's no help.
          [ROBERTO *has walked away from the table, deeply moved.*

ROBERTO. But it isn't you who ought to be in despair!
What about me, who think I can finger a pulse,
And can't even notice the racing heart-beat of someone
As near to me as you are. What's the matter with me?
I could have told you; once you had blamed yourself
You let a fear take substance, and become
An ogre of certainty, who was never there.
We all felt in some way self-accused
For Cesare's arrest—all of us.

ANA-CLARA. It was love and joy made you tell Rosa.
That's no betrayal. But when you let remorse
Wound the light in you, *then* you betrayed him.

[84]

GRAZIA. Well, we won't talk about it any more!
  I'm going for a walk!
          [GRAZIA *runs towards the archway.* ROBERTO *catches her
          as she goes.*

ROBERTO. Why didn't you help me? Wasn't I there for you?

GRAZIA. I don't want to go over it all again.
          [GIOSETTA *has made to follow, but moves into the archway
          as* ROBERTO *leads* GRAZIA *downstage.* GIOSETTA *looks
          into the street.* EDMONDO *also makes a move;* ANA-CLARA
          detains him.

ROBERTO. You don't have to, but I'm the one now
  Who needs attention.

ANA-CLARA [*to* EDMONDO]. Leave them alone.

GRAZIA. I only wish I hadn't said anything.
  I was sorry for Alfio.

ROBERTO.   What worried me
  Was whether the S.S. watched out for me
  To visit here, to be able to follow me
  Back to the hide-out; which could have been why
  They found Cesare.

GRAZIA.   Of course not; it wasn't you.

ROBERTO. We don't know. It isn't a murder mystery
  With a traceable villain. Am I to forgive you
  Or you forgive me? Or twelve other possibilities.
  We have to live with not knowing, sometimes:
  Why this man contracts a cancer, or another's
  Family burns in a house, or Cesare is taken.
  It's not your fault that the world's name is Hazard.

GRAZIA. I hope it isn't, I hope not.

ROBERTO.   Believe it.
  Can you? While we live we must expect

[85]

To be haunted, often, but not now. Help me
By not hiding.

GRAZIA.　　　　　No more secrets, I promise.
You are like this. I didn't know that.

ROBERTO.　　　　　　　　　　Odd,
What strange news we can still bring to each other.

GIOSETTA [*coming forward*]. Grazia, I want to tell you something.
We had a message today.

GRAZIA.　　　　　　About father?

ROBERTO.　　　　　　　　From Cesare?

ALFIO. Is he coming back?

　　　　　　　　[GIOSETTA *has passed the note to* GRAZIA.

GRAZIA.　　　　　Someone has seen him!
Someone has really seen him! Mother, who wrote this?

GIOSETTA. I'd say an archangel if it wasn't for the spelling.

GRAZIA. But he's coming home! Why didn't you tell me before?
What are we doing? We ought to be at the station
Ready to meet him.

GIOSETTA.　　　　But we can't say how or when—

GRAZIA. Every train, every day until he gets here!
We can sleep in the waiting-room. I'll fetch your shawl.
Why did you let so much time go by? We must
Be the first faces he sees when he comes back.

　　　　　　　　　　[GRAZIA *disappears indoors.*

ANGELINO. There, now, you have your orders.

GIOSETTA.　　　　　　　　A thousand days
Of torturing herself without telling me!
Dear God.

ANA-CLARA. It's over now. Did you ever see
Such daylight in a face as that?

[86]

GIOSETTA.   Thank goodness
  We're going down to the station anyway.
  I've been in two minds all morning and afternoon.
  I don't know why I made such a hurdle out of it.
                          [GRAZIA *comes back with the shawl.*

GRAZIA. Here you are: now let's hurry!
                [ANGELINO *and* ROBERTO *follow them into the street.*

ANGELINO.   Have a thought for your mother's legs.
  I hope the vigil won't be too wearisome.
  Bring the truant back soon.

GRAZIA.   Yes, we will!
                          [*She suddenly embraces* ROBERTO.
  I'm sorry, I'm sorry.

ROBERTO.   Goodbye. Good luck.
        [GIOSETTA *looks back, her hand on her heart, and tries to
        smile. She follows the hurrying* GRAZIA.

ALFIO [*to* EDMONDO]. Do you see what this means, if my father
    comes
  He may be here for the race—to see me ride.
  The very first time he will have seen me
  Out of a squalling cot. Do you realize?

EDMONDO. Oh, for God's sake, don't start on that again.
  It's all been settled to everyone's advantage.
  Now shut up.

ALFIO.   No, but listen. I have to show him
  I'm worth something. He put me out of his head,
  But I want him to be glad for what he fathered,
  Not ashamed of me. Surely you see that?

EDMONDO. Stop following me about. You brought it on yourself.
  You needn't think it can all be dropped
  Because you want to show off to your father.

[87]

ROBERTO. Even though it's a feeling my brother should be the first
    To appreciate.

EDMONDO.   You keep out. I'm doing this
    For the sake of the parish.

ALFIO.   Listen—

EDMONDO.   Listen to *me*—

ALFIO. No, listen, it's more than that. The only time
    I know who I am, or know I belong anywhere
    Is when I'm riding well—when I can master
    An animal stronger than I am. I know now
    Tomorrow is what my whole life has been leading up to.

EDMONDO. I'm not surprised. So it is for all of us.
    Has the other parent dropped out of your thoughts,
    Or the miracle-drug suddenly lost its virtue?

                            [ALFIO *collapses in despair*.

ALFIO. Oh, Christ, I don't know what I'm to do. I don't know.

EDMONDO. Just make your peace with necessity, my boy.

ANGELINO. Come along, come along. Don't take it so hard.

ANA-CLARA. Oh? And why shouldn't he? It *is* hard.
    It's impossibly hard. It's ethically, emotionally,
    Rationally disgustingly impossible.
    I'm on Alfio's side. I don't care about the race,
    Which was going to be all love and excitement for me,
    Not any more. What does it matter who wins?

ROBERTO. But it does matter.

ANA-CLARA.   You can tell your precious people
    It's better to lose their money than their good nature.

ROBERTO. Very compassionately said!

EDMONDO [*to* ANA-CLARA].   Since when
    Have you taken over the role of mother-goddess
    And the bleeding heart? This is a new game.

ANA-CLARA. I might teach you to play it when you have the time.

ANGELINO. How I see it, if Cesare's coming home,
The situation is different, in the nature of things.
In the nature of things.—This isn't a bad wine.
I don't know that I should drink any more, though.
—Cesare, yes, he's been going through it.
We don't want an uneasy situation
Happening here when he gets back. We should let
The boy be free to make up his own mind.

ANA-CLARA. If it isn't too late.

EDMONDO.   I give up!
I might have known it was no good trying to get
This bunkered family on to the fairway. Do
What you like with him. Chuck the race away,
If that's what you want. Don't come crying to me.

ANGELINO. Now you don't need to kick the milk-bucket over.
We appreciate what you've done—but the truth is
You tried to give us too much—that's what it was,
It all came in a flood, everything came
Together, except, somehow, us, we didn't
Come together. And that's what I looked forward to.

EDMONDO. How do you expect us to come together
When none of you knows a peach from a rotten apple?
This family! I feel I've never been out of it:
Still sixteen, and swaddled in disapproval.
As soon as I got here things began to go wrong.

ANGELINO. What an accusation! Are you holding *me*
Responsible for Cambriccio's blood-pressure?
Did I foul up the telephone wires? Did I
Split this unfortunate boy's mind
Into two equal contradictory parts?
This is how you always used to go on

D   [89]

When you got into trouble—trying to make out
Everybody else was responsible for it!

EDMONDO. I'm not saying that—I'm simply saying
Life hasn't got a chance here. I can feel
Any self-confidence draining out of me.
I knew I had made a mistake to come back home
As soon as I saw my brother's critical smirk.
He's been waiting for the chance to cut me down
To the size he first knew me.

ROBERTO.   That's not true!

EDMONDO. If not, it's because you're anxious to keep the peace
With Ana-Clara. I've no doubt you reached
Some sort of pact on the subject. Don't imagine
I haven't seen how this sentimental limbo
Has got into her bloodstream.

ANA-CLARA.   Let's not forget
This is the place you love, whatever it does to you.

ANGELINO. The afternoon turned wrongside out, that's the
    trouble.
You won't be feeling like this by the morning.

EDMONDO. If I don't, it will be all over with me.
I'll be so far into the domestic bog
I would never get out. The draggers-down
Would have power over me again, instead of me
Having some power over them. I won't chance that.
We can wait for the race, for Ana-Clara's pleasure.
We may as well bury our late hopes in style
And have the nodding plumes on the black horses.
But as soon as that's over, I'm very sorry, daddo,
We shall both be ready to leave. As a matter of fact
I've got some business to attend to in Milan.

[90]

I'll have one more go at that long-distance call.
Then you can work out the rest of life for yourselves.

[*He goes towards the Palazzo door.*

ANGELINO. If that's your judgement on us, I've nothing to say,
Not while you're in this mood; what would be the use?

ROBERTO. Look, Edmondo, if I'm your grievance—

EDMONDO.   Well, I'm yours,
And that's the fairest arrangement we can come to.

[*A man is in the archway, dressed in an odd mixture of
clothes, his feet tied up in rags. It is* CESARE SCAPARE.

ANA-CLARA. We seem to have company.

ROBERTO [*seeing him*].   What can we do for you?

[CESARE *makes a negative gesture and starts to go.*

ROBERTO. What were you wanting?

CESARE.   Nothing—I won't disturb you.

ANGELINO. Were you looking for somebody?

CESARE.   That's all right.
I thought Giosetta might be here.

ANGELINO.   Giosetta?
It isn't—Cesare? Cesare Scapare!
Why, of course! In this light I didn't know you.
What a welcome to give you, my dear, dear fellow!
We've just been talking about you.

ROBERTO.   Cesare!
I'm sorry, my mind was all over the place.
Come on, don't look such a stranger.

CESARE.   No, excuse me;
There are people here.

ANGELINO.   No people at all.
My daughter-in-law, Edmondo's wife. Come along.

[91]

Here's Edmondo himself, come home like you.
And—ah . . .

> [*He has looked uncertainly across at* ALFIO, *who shakes his
> head vigorously. But* CESARE, *after a brief nod of acknow-
> ledgement, is retreating into the archway.*

CESARE.　　　　　Excuse me. Giosetta isn't here, then?
Nor Grazia?

ANGELINO.　　It was when you smiled, I realized—
Giosetta and Grazia have gone to meet you.
You've just missed them.

CESARE.　　　　　　　I was walking about
Round the side streets, to give the years a chance
To pull themselves together. And to get to know
This man I was walking with, who could go anywhere.

ANGELINO. They haven't been gone more than five minutes.

CESARE. Are they all right?

ANGELINO.　　　　　　They will be when they find you.

CESARE. Think so? You're a hard fact to deny,
Angelino. There isn't much doubt about you.
I'll see you presently.

ANGELINO [*following him into the street*]. We shall be here.

> [*Everyone is silent. After a moment* EDMONDO *goes sharply
> into the Palazzo.* ANGELINO *comes back to the table and
> starts to clear the plates away.*

ALFIO. He wouldn't have wanted to meet me yet—even
If I had been ready for him.

ANGELINO.　　　　　Suppose you help me
Clear these things away.

> [ANA-CLARA *silently offers to help.*
> Don't lift a hand.

[92]

This, if you can believe it, was meant to be
My evening in your honour.

ANA-CLARA.   Thank you, angel.

ANGELINO. It's not one of the days when life co-operates.
                    [ANGELINO *and* ALFIO *carry the trays away.*

ALFIO. They say my mother can't live very long.
                    [*They go into the Scapare apartment.*

ROBERTO. What's it doing, this corner of the world—
Falling apart, or reshaping itself?
If Edmondo goes, do you go with him?

ANA-CLARA. It's the first time I have ever seen him afraid.

ROBERTO. Afraid? Edmondo?

ANA-CLARA.   Terrified of losing
The self-confidence that worked his wonders.
Afraid of seeing himself in the old mirror.
And now, I can see, afraid of Cesare's shadow
And the war he hasn't experienced. Afraid
Of losing the person he has worked so hard
To make a reality.

ROBERTO.   Self-glorification
Whoever suffers—do you call that a reality?

ANA-CLARA. Maybe not. I'm not sure of ours, either.
I doubt if Cesare was convinced we were real.
There may always be another reality
To make fiction of the truth we think we've arrived at.

ROBERTO. I can only imagine what Cesare's been through,
But it doesn't change my experience. On the contrary,
It plays such a livid light on to it
It screams in protest.

ANA-CLARA.   Like a political prisoner
Starved of sleep, who answers whatever you insist on.

Suppose reality isn't *what*, but *how*
You experience. Would that not contradict you?

ROBERTO. Speculation won't save us. Let's cope with what we
know about.
Are you going to sink back again into 'Mondo's world?

ANA-CLARA. Yes, I am. He gives me the patience I need
To make my mistakes, which you would never give me;
And the leisure I need to realize myself,
How far my mind, unhounded, and my free senses
Will take me, which you would never give me.

ROBERTO. So you whittle down the promise of this afternoon
To a mere biological thrust between us,
And take shelter in 'Mondo's self-delusion.

ANA-CLARA. He was real enough to make you want to show him,
Or anyway show yourself, you could take me from him.

ROBERTO. That's absolutely untrue!—Or if I did feel it
For a second, it was gone before I could act on it.

ANA-CLARA. For a second you would have used me as he has used
People, to convince himself of his strength.

ROBERTO. Do you think I would have destroyed you?

ANA-CLARA.   Yes, I do.
There was the scent of sapphire-coloured blood
That sauntered in my veins, or so you thought.
The hunt was up—to lay the donnanobile
On her back in love or confusion.

ROBERTO.   A monstrous slander!

ANA-CLARA. Is it? When I owned up to what I came from
I could see a view-halloo fade out of your eye.

ROBERTO. God protect me from a woman's intuition!
It's the one incontrovertible proof

[94]

Of spontaneous generation. You needn't think
I shall try and refute a fantasy.

ANA-CLARA.   I won't press it.
None of this has any significance
Beside the plain fact that you love Grazia.

> [ROBERTO *is silent*.

I know. I saw it take you by surprise
When you turned and rent Edmondo. You hadn't bothered
To mark its gradual height on the kitchen door.
It's much taller than you imagined, isn't it?

ROBERTO. So you say. But nevertheless—

ANA-CLARA.   I welcome that.
I could do with a nevertheless.

> [ALFIO *comes to the doorway of the Scapares'*, *drying a
> plate*.

ALFIO.   I have to tell you
I've cleared up the trouble in my mind now.
I shall ride in the race, as though this evening
Had never happened. Nothing else is possible.
I just had to banish the last two hours or so
Out of my memory. I thought I ought to warn you.

ROBERTO. I see.

> [ALFIO *goes in*.

ANA-CLARA.   Nevertheless?

ROBERTO.   What we found in each other—

> LUIGI *enters from the street*.

LUIGI. Well, that's the introduction over. I let him
Get to know the pressure of my knees
Against his rib-barrel. A beautiful creature,
But as nervous as I am. Did Edmondo fix it?

ROBERTO. Yes, he fixed it.

[95]

LUIGI.   Where are they all?

ROBERTO. Cesare has come back.

LUIGI.   No? By God,
Has he? Is he all right?

ROBERTO.   I didn't recognize him.

LUIGI. Really? Remember how I told you yesterday
The starting-gun had gone off? It's not a bad omen.
What with the heat and anxiety, I'm exhausted.
There's a snake of lightning twitching low on the hills
Towards Arezzo. The storm is still around somewhere.
Well, a drink, a wash, and then home for a night's rest.

                          [LUIGI *goes into the Osteria.*

ROBERTO. We won't tell him about Alfio.
Let's leave him in good heart, as long as we can.

ANA-CLARA. Yes, why not?—I wonder what sort of heart
Edmondo is in. It's time I went to find out.
As for me, I reflected the light behind your head
And made you turn to look.

ROBERTO.   These two days,
Can I tell you what they meant?

                    LUIGI *re-emerges.*

LUIGI.   There's water in the taps,
Did you know? Arterial red, like the Tiber.
I'll leave it running and see if it comes clear.

                          [*He goes back inside.*

ANA-CLARA. Nevertheless will do. It's a river word
Flowing past and never leaving. Sleep soundly.
There's a challenging day tomorrow.

ROBERTO.   And you, too.
          [*The light swiftly fades to darkness. In the dark, the sound,
          gradually increasing, of an excited crowd, the emphatic*

[96]

*ringing of the bell in the campanile. A gunshot. The roar of
the crowd as the race begins. Above the dark stage light
strikes on rippling banners.*

[*The light returns to show* CESARE *at his doorway listening
to the noise. A gunshot signals the end of the race.*

[*It is the next afternoon.* CESARE *is neat and shaven.
A number is tattooed on his forearm. He calls back into the
house.*

CESARE. That's it, Giosetta!

GIOSETTA [*off*]. All over, is it?

CESARE. It's all over. You're either richer or poorer.

GIOSETTA. I should like to know which.

CESARE. Haven't you a premonition?

GIOSETTA *comes out to him.*

GIOSETTA. Is it likely? If I was given to premonitions
Those shunting trucks would have shaken me silly
All these weeks you were trying to get back here.

CESARE. You should have gone down and seen what was happening.

GIOSETTA. Don't imagine you're the only one
Who doesn't like being buried alive in his neighbours.

CESARE. I'll get back to them, but the herding is over
Thank God.—After you had gone to sleep
I tried breathing in rhythm with your breathing.
I wasn't far out. But it kept me awake
And I gave up.
            [*He laughs, kisses her, and sits on a stone seat by the wall.*
            If Alfio has won
He is going to be disappointed I wasn't there.

[97]

GIOSETTA. And relieved if he lost. Don't let that worry you.
You met last night like two donkeys
Eating a thorn-bush to get at the grass.
You don't have to *earn* each other.

CESARE.   It's all
Given away free with the daylight, you mean? . . .
When we crossed the Brenner we all knew where we were
Even though it was still dark. We started to sing
But couldn't keep it up. You never know
How many disguises fear can take.
This one took me off my guard. A kind of
Rising panic to find myself without
Anything to fear. It was almost comic.
Dropped into life, after so long in a place
Where life was like a belief in the supernatural.

[GIOSETTA *sits beside him on the seat.*

CESARE. Then coming down from Verona in the daylight—
The farms, the people going about the roads,
They kept coming at me like waves of pain:
I seemed to be forcing them out of me
And the muscles were cramped with not being used.
If anyone ever asks you
Who gave birth to Venezia and Emilia
You can tell them I did.

GIOSETTA.   I'll remember that.

CESARE. Just as well you weren't at the station, both of you.
When I got down, my legs were trembling and sprawling
Like a calf some cow had just dropped.
Not seeing you I felt lost, and then thankful,
And then so horrified, remembering
I didn't know what had happened to you, my legs
Ran me down the platform as though I had seen you.

[98]

GIOSETTA. You coming to look for us was a good way
   Of finding you.

CESARE [*laughing*]. The time it took, after I shouted,
   Before your faces exploded!

GIOSETTA.   Don't imagine
   I didn't know you. There wasn't a second
   When I didn't know you. You can beg my pardon.

CESARE. All right, but, I'll tell you, I was thankful
   To get that first look over, and you started to laugh.

GIOSETTA. You looked such a rag-man, I never saw the equal!
                     [CESARE *leans his head back against the wall.*

CESARE. A good idea, the sun.

GIOSETTA.   Yes, it helps.

CESARE. When do you think I ought to tell Grazia
   What I'm thinking of doing?
                     [GIOSETTA *doesn't speak for a few moments.* CESARE *takes*
                     her hand.

GIOSETTA.   Before Alfio gets here
   Or anything's decided. Talk it out
   As you and I did, so that she can understand.

CESARE. It's not easy to talk of half-seen ghosts by sunlight.
                     [GRAZIA *runs in from the street,* ROBERTO *follows more*
                     slowly.

GRAZIA. Here we are!

GIOSETTA.   Well, let's hear the worst, then.

GRAZIA. I'm not to tell you, Angelino says;
   He wants to be first with the news.

ROBERTO.   We're sworn to be silent.

GIOSETTA. It isn't fair. Why did you trouble to run, then?

[99]

GRAZIA. To see my father, who is better than any horse race.
How does the morning find you today, silent one?
[*She has sat beside him, and puts her head on his shoulder.*

CESARE. With such treasure stored up for me, in a daughter
And her mother, I want the key to their kingdom.

GRAZIA. Something is troubling you, isn't it?

CESARE.   I've got to re-learn
The skill of being earth-borne, which I was never
Much of a hand at. You may have to forgive
The laborious apprentice. As it happens
There's a place prepared for a beginner in Naples
If Alfio's mother and Alfio will accept me.

GRAZIA. Oh, no!

CESARE.   You see, I have to find my way.
And easing the sting of death in the next bunk
Is something I know about. It will give me a chance
To feel less at sea with the run of the world.

GRAZIA. No, I won't understand, I won't give you up!
We can't let him go, can we?

GIOSETTA.   Not easily,
None of it is easy.

GRAZIA.   You tell him, Roberto,
How soon we can mend the world for him here.

ROBERTO. You can't say what anyone had better do.
As we very well saw just now at the race.

GRAZIA [*laughing in spite of herself*].   That's true!

GIOSETTA. Don't tease us!

GRAZIA [*to* CESARE].   I deserve to be without you
After what I did.

[100]

CESARE.   Oh, daughter, where's your promise
  That you would never have such thoughts again?
  Moonshine. One wincing member of the family
  Is enough. You have to be my maker of quiet.
  Ask Roberto. What good's a healer for a neighbour
  If you don't make use of him?

ROBERTO.   Ah, what good *is* he?

CESARE. Ask Grazia.

GIOSETTA.   If we're all going to live
  By asking questions, here comes the answer
  To one of mine.
          Enter ANGELINO, ANA-CLARA, *and* EDMONDO
                    Angelino, tell us,
  Take us out of our misery, out with it.

ANGELINO. What an experience! We shall never live through
  The like of that again!

ANA-CLARA.   Or we shouldn't survive it.

ANGELINO. Alfio rode like a perfect master.

GIOSETTA.   I see—
  So it was Alfio, as we all thought it would be.

ANGELINO. No, no, no, he didn't win. We won.

GIOSETTA. We won? Are you serious?

ROBERTO.   Yes, he's quite serious.
  Isn't he, Grazia?

ANGELINO.   I always said
  Luigi was the one to succeed. All he needed
  Was the opportunity.

GIOSETTA.   I can't understand it.
  If Alfio rode so well, how did Luigi beat him?

ANGELINO. How? It doesn't matter how.

ROBERTO.   Of course it matters.
That was the brilliant part of it. He fell off.

GIOSETTA. Fell off?

ANA-CLARA.   And of course I thought Alfio had won.
I couldn't imagine why they were all throwing
Their arms round each other's necks in an ecstasy—
Till they said if the horse comes in, the race is won,
Never mind what happened to the man.

GRAZIA.   The horse was so happy
Not to have Luigi on him, he flew past Alfio
Right on the last corner like a bird.

ANA-CLARA. It was a miracle!

ROBERTO.   The miracle would have been
If Luigi had stayed on. But nature rallied.

EDMONDO. He nearly came off in the first two yards,
But he clung on like a crab for a circuit and a half
And fell off when he angled at the San Martino.

ANA-CLARA. I hardly had time to scream before he was up
On his feet and clear of the track.

ROBERTO.   With Luigi's bounce
It's odd he didn't land straight back on the horse.

GIOSETTA. It's a shame to mock him.

ANGELINO.   We don't want him to feel
Discomforted after such a victory.
What we must do is show him we're celebrating.
He can't help it if things didn't turn out
Quite as he planned them; that's the world for you.
                              [*He goes into the Osteria.*

EDMONDO. For some people it may be. If you like
To travel standing about thumbing a lift

And then do most of the distance on foot.
Nobody ever made a future that way.

CESARE. How is it made?

EDMONDO.   What do you mean?

CESARE.   I was wondering
Just what state of mind gives us a future.
I suppose you mean the future; not the present
Made more bearable or more efficient.
What's the good if it's not a difference in kind?
There's not a lot we know can be called the future.

EDMONDO. I'm talking about taking care of tomorrow,
Cesare.

CESARE. Oh, tomorrow, the next man's present.
I thought you were talking about something more cheerful,
A revolution.

EDMONDO.   Revolution? That's Roberto's province.

CESARE. No, no. I mean the real revolution,
The transformation.

ROBERTO.   I don't know what's in your mind.
If we get the conditions straight the rest will follow.

CESARE. The rest of what? That's what I'm asking.
Where does the mind go next, in your well-cared-for
System of being born and being buried?
I haven't your simple faith that a man can be doctored
Out of his tragedy into the millennium.

ROBERTO. God knows you've got every reason to feel
The human experiment has failed. But I promise, Cesare,
We're not going to forget what happened to you.

CESARE. Failed? That's not it. I never set
So much value on us as I do now,

[103]

Heart, mind, and vision: all we can call human,
Not wolf, jackal, vulture, and pig.
In the camp, you don't know what utopias
We built out of some flicker of humanity.
How, in what way, won't you forget?
Don't, for God's sake, reward us
By staring so long at the gorgon's head
It grips the muscles of your living face.
We've been in the dirt. We don't want to be remembered
By generations playing at mud-pies
And calling it the true image of life—
I'd rather come soon to the clean skull.
Purify us, Roberto, purify us!
Insist on all the powers that recover us!

GRAZIA. But, father, what has he said, what's the matter?

CESARE. I was getting excited. That was a shouting
Out of the old nights before I got back to you.
> [*A sound of chanting and cheering, growing louder.*
> ANGELINO *comes back with a tray of wine and glasses.*

ANGELINO. Here we are, all ready for the conqueror.
We won't have Luigi thinking he's disgraced himself.
Let's hope that he hasn't slunk away somewhere.
We want him with us.

EDMONDO.   By the sound of it
You're going to have him.

ANGELINO.   Did you hear that?
They're shouting my name. What a morning to have lived for!
> [*Into the archway comes a group of* MEN *in fifteenth-century
> costume, carrying* LUIGI, *in his jockey cap and shirt, in
> triumph on their shoulders. They bear him once round the
> courtyard, chanting:*

MEN.   B-R-U-N-O, BRUNO!
              Who is Bruno? You know Bruno!
              Bruno son of Angelino.
              Luigi Bruno the fantino!
              B-R-U-N-O, BRUNO!
        [*As the chanting stops* LUIGI *jumps down and embraces*
        ANGELINO.

LUIGI. I've done it! I've done it! I've brought it off!

ANGELINO. Bravo, you have, I knew that you could do it.

LUIGI. I've put us on the map, haven't I, eh?

ANGELINO. Bruno, son of Angelino—what a triumph!
        [LUIGI *goes round embracing everybody; he dances* GRAZIA
        in his arms; kisses ANA-CLARA.

LUIGI. Well, there, was it anything like the vision you had?

ANA-CLARA. Yes, and beyond. I was lifted off the earth.

LUIGI. That wasn't what it did to me.—Giosetta,
  You'd be proud of me, if you thought of me at all
  Now Cesare's home. And here is the man himself.
  You see what I go through to give you a welcome.

CESARE. Well done. Give my compliments to the horse.

LUIGI. How was that, Bobo? I just gave life a chance
  To find her own way.—There, 'Mondo, you see,
  I wasn't such a bad substitute after all.

ANGELINO. I propose the health of the man who saved the parish.
        [*Calls of 'Luigi!' from the* MEN *and the others.*

EDMONDO. This is the moment to tell you what's in my mind.
  As Ana-Clara and I won't need the Palazzo
  I intend to make it into a restaurant:
  Angelino's, the paradise of gourmets,
  The shrine of pilgrim gastronomes, the goal

[105]

Of epicures. We'll have a gala opening
With everyone here who counts for anything.
The rest of the world will follow like sheep to be fed.
You'll prosper all right, daddo. It will be as easy—
I was going to say as falling off a horse,
But I don't want to reflect on Luigi's success.

[ROBERTO *has given a private groan.*

LUIGI. Learn by it, 'Mondo dear. You've cast a gloom
Over Bobo again. Drink up, boys. We haven't
Finished the lap of triumph yet. Are you ready?
This was only a wayside halt in our progress.

[*The* MEN *thank* ANGELINO *for the wine and hoist* LUIGI
*on to their shoulders. They march out into the street, taking
up their chant of* 'B-R-U-N-O! BRUNO!' ANGELINO
follows them as far as the street. CESARE, GIOSETTA,
GRAZIA, *and* ROBERTO *are laughing.*

GIOSETTA. I needn't have been anxious about his feelings!

ROBERTO. There won't be any holding him now.

ANA-CLARA.   Except
That you can't fall off a horse every day of your life.

CESARE. I think Luigi could. And if there aren't any shoulders
To ride on, he will find a way to invent them.

ANGELINO *comes back from the street.*

ANGELINO. He has turned the whole district into heroes.
They all think they could have done it themselves,
Cheering themselves like champions. They don't realize
It takes Luigi's particular ability.

GIOSETTA. Has anyone been to see Cambriccio?

ROBERTO. Yes, I went with Grazia. He's doing all right.

EDMONDO. What do you say about the restaurant, daddo?

[106]

It's what you've always wanted, isn't it?
The day's come round, to see things turn into gold.

ANGELINO. Yes, I appreciate that.

EDMONDO.   Appreciate it!
Well, I hope you do.

ANA-CLARA [*to* CESARE]. I'm still thinking
About the future you see for us, as if
Our variation to adapt to life
Was hardly begun.—All through the afternoon
I felt as though the barriers were breaking
Between our world and another.

                              [CESARE *has withdrawn into himself.*

EDMONDO [*to* ANGELINO].   Can't you think
Of anything more to say than that?

ROBERTO [*to* ANA-CLARA].   The old
Stimulant: bells, trumpets, drums, flag-juggling,
It's a heady mixture. It comes very near
Even to seducing me, and I'm used to it!

ANGELINO [*to* EDMONDO]. I shall turn it over in my mind, of
    course,
Of course.

EDMONDO. Turn it over? What does that mean?
Isn't it good enough? I don't understand.

ANA-CLARA. It's a great slow love-making, anyway,
And left me vibrating like an instrument.
So nearly the city had no need of the sun
Or the moon to shine on it. I could almost see
By the light that streamed from the trumpets
And shimmered from the bell. The courting sun-birds,
The birds of paradise, so nearly sang
The indwelling music which created us.

[107]

ANGELINO [*to* EDMONDO]. I seem to be full of misgivings.

EDMONDO.   You're impossible!
   Hopeless!

ROBERTO [*to* ANA-CLARA]. You have to feed your bird of paradise
   If you want it to sing.

ANGELINO [*to* EDMONDO]. When I start to think
   Of all those mouths opening and shutting,
   Chewing on my efforts to please, day in, day out,
   I feel discouraged at the prospect. I don't believe
   I could love them, even on closing day.

EDMONDO [*outraged*]. Please yourself. Don't say I haven't tried.
   Ana-Clara, it's time we got going.

ANA-CLARA.   I won't be long.
                                   [EDMONDO *goes into the Palazzo.*

ANGELINO. I don't know whether I'm a greater disappointment
   To 'Mondo or to me. I like to enjoy
   A glittering prospect, but not to the extent
   Of letting it take you over body and soul.
   I draw the line there. It's one rule of conduct
   I *can* say that I've got.

ANA-CLARA.   I could stay and talk
   All night, and rivet the stars with attention,
   About what we are, to ourselves and to each other,
   What things destroy us and what things create—
   They are better guides than any rule-book,
   Though as intricate as a meeting of waters.
   But it's not to be now: all for some other evening.

ANGELINO. Now that's what I like to hear you say—
   That makes me more cheerful.

GRAZIA [*with her arm round* CESARE]. Some other evening

When we're all together again. I wonder
How we are going to get on until then.

                [ROBERTO *looks at his watch and moves away.*

ROBERTO. I don't know what I'm doing sitting about here.
I've some calls to make.

CESARE.   Blessed the profession
Where a man's meaning is plain.

ROBERTO [*suddenly turning*].   Ah! But would you
Trust your daughter to me?

GIOSETTA.   About as much
As I trust life, which is every now and again.

ANGELINO. Have you found your way to asking her, at last?
I knew you were the one with the intelligence.
If you mean to get married you will have to find
Some patients who can pay you. What a mercy!

GRAZIA. Angelino, he hasn't asked me anything.
You mustn't start prospecting again.

ANGELINO.   Oh, mustn't I?

ROBERTO. We'll see what we can do. Don't lose heart.
      [*He goes into the Osteria. A procession emerges from the
      Palazzo: the* THREE MENSERVANTS, *the* LADY'S MAID,
      the SECRETARY, *the* CHAUFFEUR *carrying luggage. They
      go towards the archway.*

ANA-CLARA. Here's my wagon-train moving off. And I must fall
Into step behind them.

                  [*She goes to the Palazzo doorway.*

ANGELINO.   The poor empty Palazzo.

ANA-CLARA. Suppose Edmondo started a clinic here?
How do you think Roberto would feel about that?

        [*A scream of motor-cycle brakes outside in the street.*

[109]

CESARE. With an accident ward for the unlucky.

GIOSETTA. It sounds like Alfio again.

ANA-CLARA.   And it is Alfio.

> [ALFIO *wheels his machine in through the archway.*

ANGELINO. We thought it was you. Why don't you look where you're going?

> [ALFIO *grins, and gives the extravagant Neopolitan gesture he gave before, but this time ironically.* CESARE *makes the same gesture in sympathetic reply. The others are laughing*

and THE CURTAIN FALLS

A NOTE ON THE PALIO

by STEWART PEROWNE

(Reprinted by permission of *The Times*)

THE contest is of great antiquity. The accounts relating to it are extant for the year 1347, that is more than a century before the eclipse of Byzantium, between which and Siena, Duccio and his school had already forged such compelling pictorial links. The Palio (so-called from the painted cloth representing the Madonna which is the prize) restores to us twice a year, on the 2nd July and the 16th August, not only the galvanic hazard of the hippodrome, but the dazzling liturgy of life as well. In Byzantium these were inseparable; to-day only very rarely, as at the Palio, are they to be enjoyed together.

The competitors are representative of ten of the seventeen *contrade*, or wards, into which Siena is divided. They are not performers: this, for them, is an aspect of life. Every son of Siena when he is baptized becomes not only a child of God but a member of his *contrada* too. All his life he will remain one, and though he dwell in foreign lands for many years, if he returns to Siena, it is to his own ward that he will go back. Each ward has its own emblem. In 1969, for instance, the competitors bore the following: the snail, the tortoise, the scallop, the caterpillar, the unicorn, the giraffe, the goat, the panther, the wolf and the eagle, bicephalous and Byzantine. The proceedings take place in the *campo*, the mediaeval piazza which is dominated by the *Palazzo Pubblico*. It has something of the shape of a strung bow, so that the course, over cobbles sanded and boarded for the occasion, contains two corners, one at the beginning, the other at the end of a sharp declivity, comparable to the hairpin bends at the ends of the axis of a Roman race-course.

The proceedings open with a grand procession called the *corteo*, which for two hours circles the *campo* in solemn pageant. First come beadles shouldering maces, followed by a standard-bearer holding the *Balzana*, the argent and sable blazon of the City, twelve trumpeters, the gonfalon of Montalcino 'by ancient custom', and thirty-five citizens bearing the banners of the 'cities, mayoralties, vicariates, lands and castles which make up the state of Siena'. The standard-bearer of the court-merchant comes next, with three magistrates carrying the statutes of the corporations

[111]

inscribed on rolls of parchment. Then come the banners of the corporations themselves, the workers in silk, wool, and stone, the painters, goldsmiths, apothecaries and blacksmiths, followed by two hundred members of the corporations. The Captain of the people, attended and mounted, precedes what is the heart of the display, the *contrade* each represented by a drummer, two *alfieri*, or flag-carriers, the *Duce* in full armour and flanked by men-at-arms equipped with bows or halberds, a page bearing the achievement of the *contrada*, and two others carrying banners. Then on a sturdy war-horse comes the jockey (the only professional in the whole parade) followed by his race-horse led by a groom.

Solemnly the groups circle the thronged arena. All are clad in the style of the *quattrocento*, the garb of each changed and counterchanged according to its heraldic bearings. The effect is prismatically enthralling. The brocades are rigid with gold, the velvets shimmer in the westering sun. The whole array recalls the processions of Benozzo Gozzoli, or his contemporaries Cossa and Verrocchio. Little Tobias in our National Gallery might have stepped right out of the Palio. Or straight back into it; because the remarkable thing about the display is its complete naturalness. These lads (few are over thirty) are not players: they are, not act, what we see. There is not a whiff of Wardour Street about it. Here for a day the Middle Age has become *primavera*, first youth.

The companies progress, until there are six or seven of them girdling the *campo*. Up shoot the flags, dextrously launched and caught by the two *alfieri* of each *contrada*, spangling the blue sky with their rich hues, from the primrose and gold of the Eagle to the amaranth of the Elephant, which with the six other non-competitors, goose, dragon, rhinoceros, owl, dolphin and porcupine bring up the rear. Finally, tumultuously acclaimed, comes the gilded car, hauled by four white oxen, which carries the Palio itself. While this is making its honorific round, its penitential bell a-tinkling, the jockeys doff their finery and reappear in lighter garments and close-fitting caps. With nervous dignity they find their allotted places between the starting ropes. They ride bareback.

Some of the horses have appeared before, so have many of the riders; but the peculiar hazards of the course make the Palio the tensest three minutes in contemporary racing. The double circuit is watched by an audience which in numbers equals that of the Verona amphitheatre, itself the modern representative of Rome's Colosseum, but in excitement far exceeds it. Every window of the ancient palaces is a vantage-point. For the climax even the date-panel on the campanile clock is replaced by eager heads. Down below, the *campo* is packed with faces which form a mosaic far more eloquent than any tessellated record from antiquity. The great bell tolls unheard above the human thunder, the pigeons circle un-harboured and unheeded. Only the horses and their riders are there for the spectators, who by their emotion become fused into participation.

To participate, to belong, to be. If anything is still left remarkable beneath the visited moon, here it is man himself, who in Siena can still surpass, in appeal and impact, the most splendid shadows of Verona's operas.